ODILON REDON

Otherworldly Visions

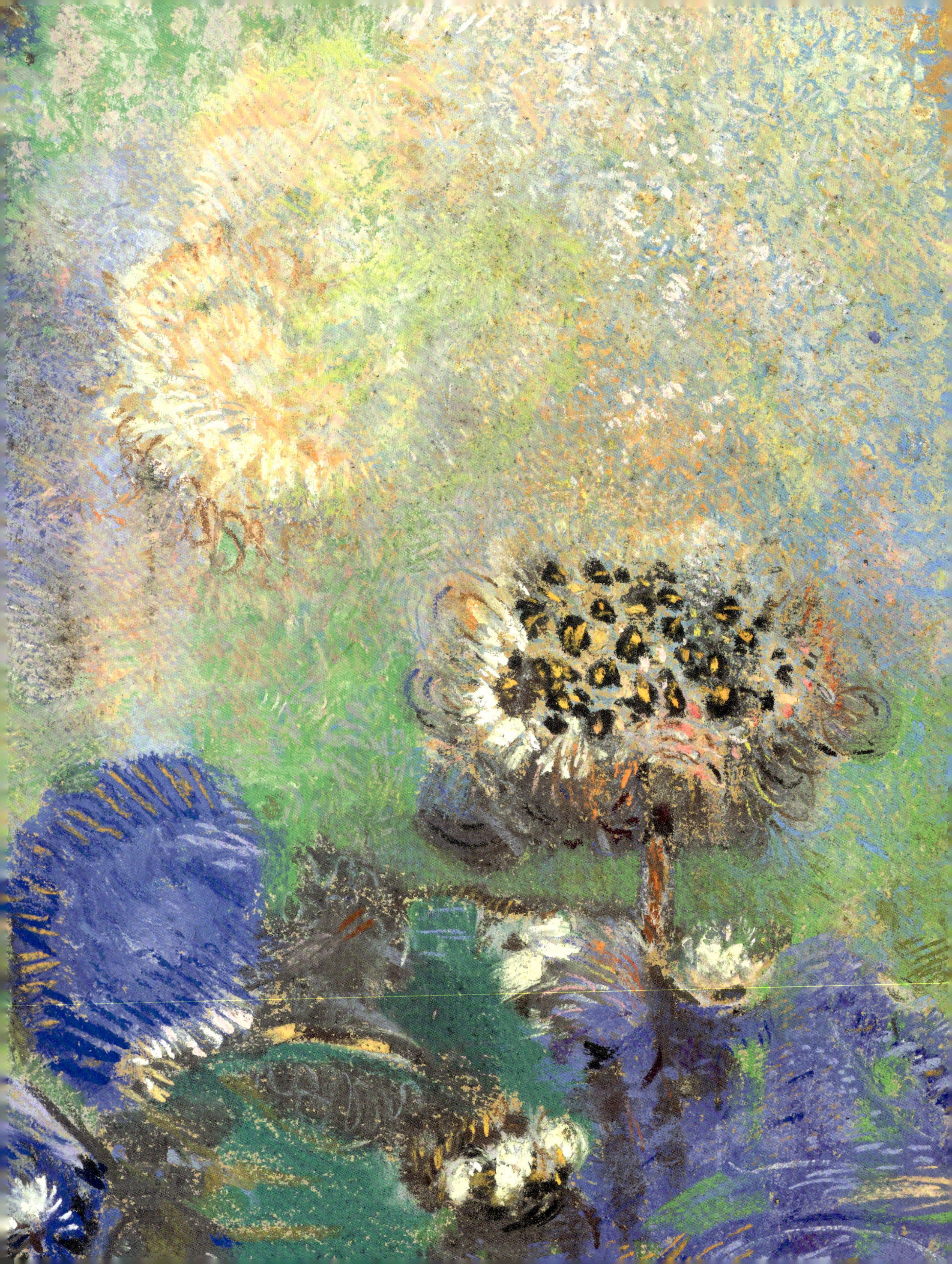

ODILON REDON

OTHERWORLDLY VISIONS

Danielle Canter

with

Natalia Lauricella

J. Paul Getty Museum, Los Angeles

This publication is issued on the occasion of the exhibition *Odilon Redon: Otherworldly Visions*, on view at the J. Paul Getty Museum at the Getty Center, Los Angeles, from July 14 to October 18, 2026.

Published by the J. Paul Getty Museum, Los Angeles
Getty Publications
1200 Getty Center Drive, Suite 500
Los Angeles, California 90049-1682
getty.edu/publications

Nikki Bazar and Ruth Evans Lane, *Project Editors*
Nikki Bazar, *Manuscript Editor*
Jon Grizzle, *Designer*
Michelle Deemer, *Production*
Danielle Brink, *Image and Rights Acquisition*

Distributed in the United States and Canada by the University of Chicago Press

Distributed outside the United States and Canada by Yale University Press, London

Printed in China

Library of Congress Cataloging-in-Publication Data
Names: Canter, Danielle, author. | Lauricella, Natalia, contributor. | Redon, Odilon, 1840–1916. | J. Paul Getty Museum, host institution, issuing body.
Title: Odilon Redon : otherworldly visions / Danielle Canter with Natalia Lauricella.
Other titles: Otherworldly visions
Description: Los Angeles : J. Paul Getty Museum, [2026] | Published on the occasion of an exhibition at the J. Paul Getty Museum in Los Angeles. | Includes bibliographical references and index. | Summary: "Including over 70 images, this catalogue, which accompanies an exhibition at the J. Paul Getty Museum in Los Angeles, offers an accessible introduction to the work of the French Symbolist artist Odilon Redon, from his early experiments in printmaking to his later richly hued pastels" — Provided by publisher.
Identifiers: LCCN 2026002275 | ISBN 9798887120188 (paperback) | ISBN 9798887120195 (epub) | ISBN 9798887120201 (adobe pdf)
Subjects: LCSH: Redon, Odilon, 1840–1916—Exhibitions. | Symbolism (Art movement)—France—Exhibitions. | LCGFT: Exhibition catalogs.
Classification: LCC N6853.R38 A4 2026
LC record available at https://lccn.loc.gov/2026002275

Cover: Detail of *The Battle of the Bones* (plate 2)
p. ii: Detail of *Baronne de Domecy* (plate 43)
p. vi: Detail of *Then There Appears a Singular Being, Having the Head of a Man on the Body of a Fish* (plate 12)
p. 12: Detail of *Head Within an Aureole* (plate 38)
p. 28: Detail of *Light* (plate 5)

Illustration Credits
Every effort has been made to contact the owners and photographers of illustrations reproduced here whose names do not appear in the captions or in the illustration credits listed at the back of this book. Anyone having further information concerning copyright holders is asked to contact Getty Publications so this information can be included in future printings.

The captions in this volume use sheet dimensions for the artworks, unless otherwise indicated.

Quotations
Page 53 ("new monsters"): Redon 1923, 32
Page 65 ("infinitely small," "imperceptible world"): Redon 1986 [1922], 14

Authorized Product Safety Representative in the European Union: Easy Access System Europe, Mustamäe tee 50, 10621 Tallinn, Estonia, gpsr.requests@easproject.com

MIX
Paper | Supporting responsible forestry
FSC® C008047

Contents

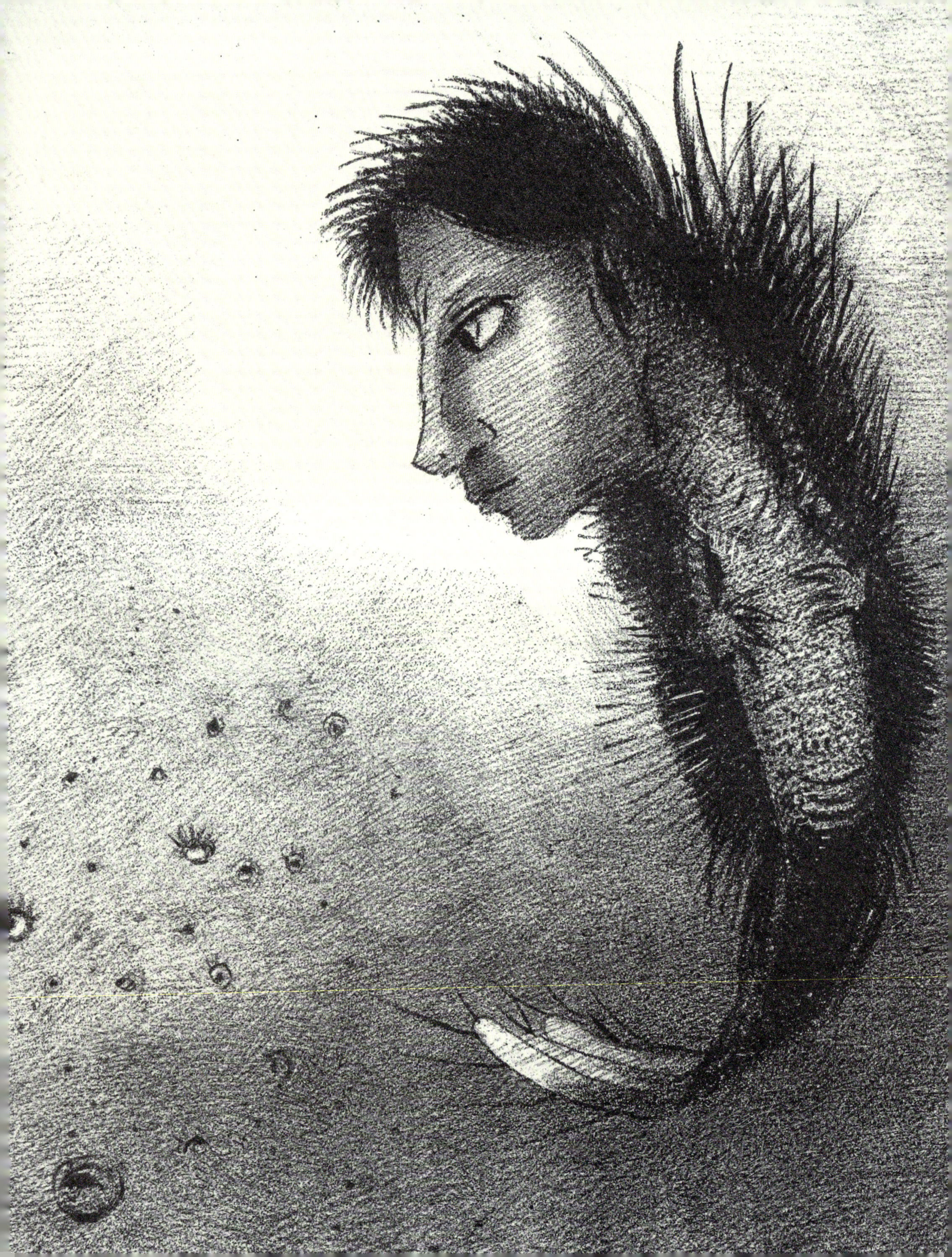

Foreword

Born the same year as Claude Monet and Auguste Rodin, Odilon Redon (French, 1840–1916) lived during a period of boundless innovation in French art, to which he contributed greatly through the creation of a distinctively visionary world of fantasy and imagination, manifested in a wide-ranging oeuvre of drawings, prints, and paintings. Even as he thrived in this rich environment, however, Redon stood apart from Post-Impressionists, Symbolists, and members of other fin-de-siècle movements with his otherworldly depictions of radiant dreams and shadowy nightmares. Whether because of this imagery, his eschewal of movements, or both, Redon does not today enjoy the broad public renown that many of his contemporaries posthumously attained. His singular visual imagination, however, has had an extraordinary impact on artists, from the early twentieth-century Surrealists to those working in the present day, and has won him a cult following also among art lovers, collectors, and scholars.

Odilon Redon: Otherworldly Visions is the first in-depth presentation of Redon's art on the West Coast of the United States. It serves to introduce visitors to the artist's profound originality and offers many new insights into his working practice and reception. Although he spent his entire life in France, Redon had strong ties to North America. His parents met and married in New Orleans, relocating to France only weeks before his birth, and these distant origins figured prominently in his self-identity. At the Armory Show of 1913, the first major exhibition of European modernism in the United States, no artist had more works represented than Redon. The subsequent critical acclaim contributed to the significant body of his work that now resides in American collections.

Indeed, this exhibition and the accompanying publication highlight the excellent group of charcoal drawings, pastels, and prints by Redon in the collections of the J. Paul Getty Museum and the Getty Research Institute. In 2024 the Getty Museum augmented these holdings with the purchase of *The Battle of the Bones*, a quintessentially enigmatic charcoal *noir* (as the artist termed it) drawing that epitomizes Redon's technical skill and macabre sense of humor. In addition, we have supplemented the exhibition with loans from fellow California institutions: the Fine Arts Museums of San Francisco, the Hammer Museum, the Los Angeles County Museum of Art, and the Santa Barbara Museum of Art. We are deeply grateful to these lenders, whose generous contributions allow us to represent the broader scope of Redon's remarkable career.

I offer thanks to Danielle Canter, assistant curator of drawings, for bringing the exhibition and this engaging catalogue to fruition. Through the lens of Redon's innovative materials and techniques, the essays in this book offer new perspectives on the artist's strange and extraordinary world. I have no doubt that visitors and readers will be intrigued and inspired by the art of Redon and his unique creative vision.

Timothy Potts
Maria Hummer-Tuttle and Robert Tuttle Director
J. Paul Getty Museum

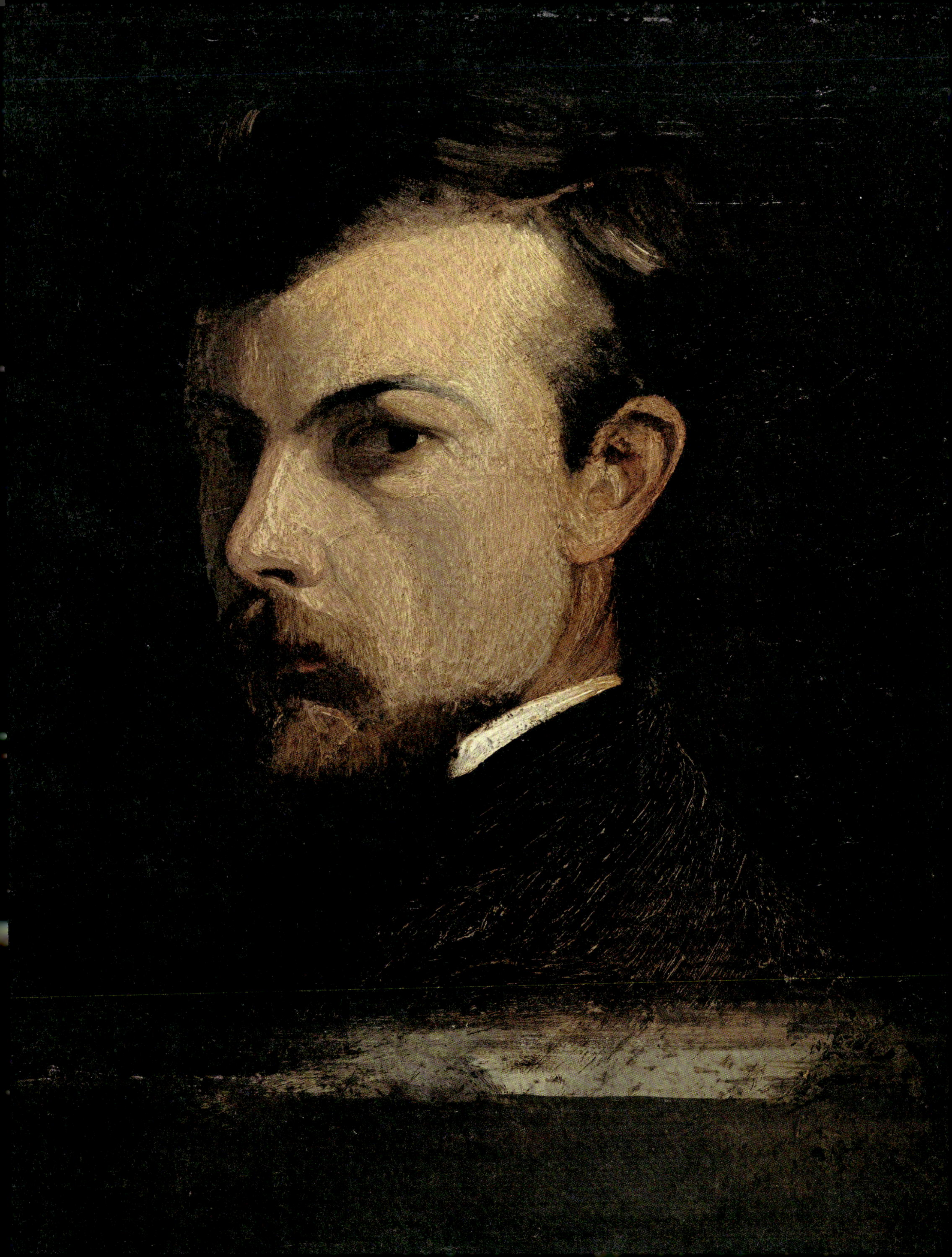

Introduction

Danielle Canter

To view the art of Odilon Redon is to enter another world. Drawing on the observed and the imagined, Redon created his own fantastical realm filled with mysterious apparitions and strange monsters. Although his career coincided with many of the major art movements in nineteenth-century France, he remains a singular figure (fig. 1). True to his own vision, he refused to adhere to any one group and steadfastly resisted attempts to decipher or elucidate his work. Reflecting on his career in a letter to a friend, he declared emphatically, "I have made an art according to myself."[1] Redon used his art to offer new interpretations of the familiar, rendering literary, biblical, and mythical subjects in original ways. He also found inspiration in nature, merging modern science and the imagination to depict hybrid creatures and surreal flora in his drawings, prints, and paintings.

Although Redon's strange and enigmatic art may seem drawn from an unreal world, his work was grounded in his lived experience and the cultural environment of late nineteenth- and early twentieth-century France. Born in 1840 in Bordeaux, Redon was isolated for most of his childhood due to persistent illness, sent to live with a distant relative at the family's country estate. The haunting imagery of the artist's oeuvre is often assumed to originate from his lonely youth in the countryside, where he communed with nature and took "singular and profound joy in hiding among the great curtains in dark corners of the house."[2] As a young man, Redon had an interest in painting but also pursued music

FIG. 1 Odilon Redon (French, 1840–1916), *My Portrait*, 1867. Oil on wood, 41.7 × 32 cm (16 7⁄16 × 12 5⁄8 in.). Paris, Musée d'Orsay, Bequest of Mrs. Arï Redon in execution of the wishes of her husband, son of Odilon Redon, 1982, RF 1984 39

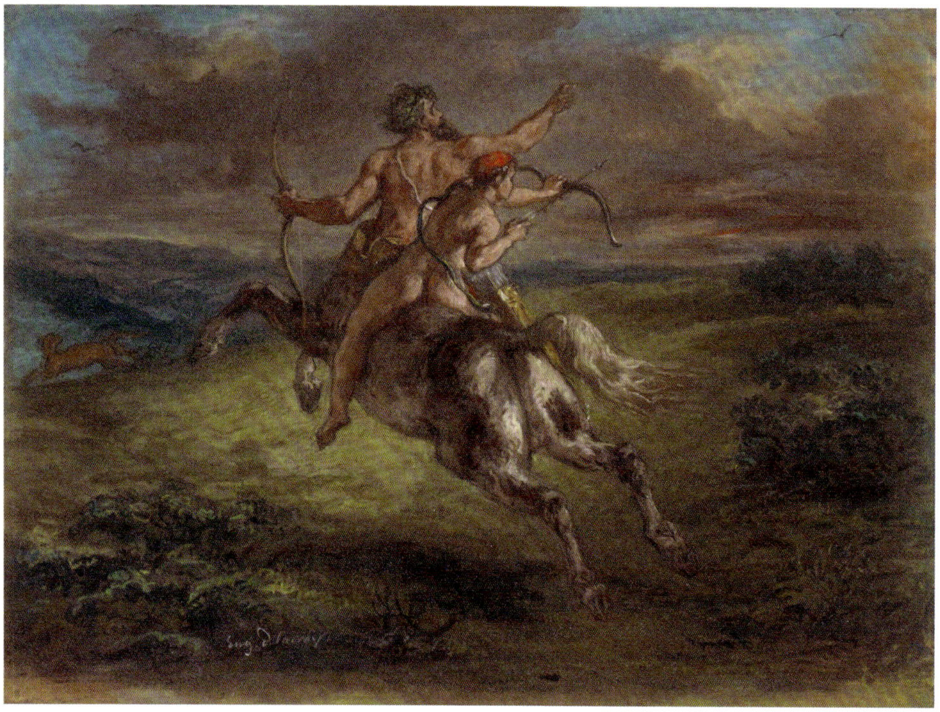

FIG. 2 Eugène Delacroix (French, 1798–1863), *The Education of Achilles*, 1862. Pastel, 30.6 × 41.9 cm (12 1/16 × 16 1/2 in.). Los Angeles, J. Paul Getty Museum, 86.GG.728. This drawing is a later version Delacroix made of his original composition.

and architecture at the behest of his father before deciding to focus on visual art. Despite this circuitous career path, his early years were spent discovering many of the artistic and literary influences that he would retain throughout his life. In Bordeaux, he developed a close friendship with the botanist Armand Clavaud, who helped to inspire his enduring interest in the representation of plant life. A bohemian figure with varied pursuits, Clavaud also introduced Redon to a broad array of subjects that he would later incorporate into his art, including modern evolutionary science, Eastern philosophy, and the writings of Edgar Allan Poe. The two shared a great admiration for the colorful and emotional art of the Romantic painter Eugène Delacroix, whom Redon viewed as a spiritual mentor. He found particular inspiration in Delacroix's *The Education of Achilles* (fig. 2), a striking depiction of the human form in motion, which Redon copied in a drawing that he prized throughout his life.[3]

Though Redon did not have the opportunity to study directly with Delacroix, he sought to hone his skills under the instruction of other established artists. He studied briefly and unproductively under the Academic painter Jean-Léon Gérôme in Paris in 1864 before returning to Bordeaux and training in printmaking with Rodolphe Bresdin,

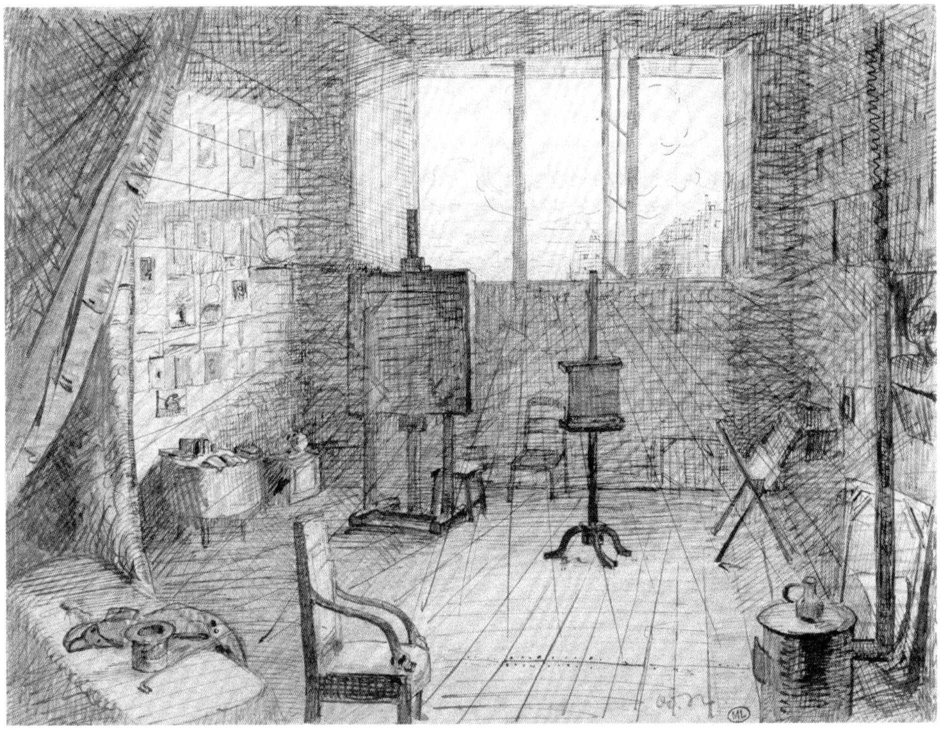

FIG. 3 Odilon Redon, *The Studio of Redon* (recto), ca. 1875. Graphite, pen, and ink, 17.8 × 23.8 cm (7 × 9 ⅜ in.). Paris, Musée du Louvre, Gift of Arï et Suzanne Redon, 1982, RF 40857

a self-taught artist known for his intricate and eccentric landscape etchings (see fig. 19). Despite this tutelage, Redon struggled to define his artistic voice and found limited success in the 1860s Bordeaux art scene. His nascent career was interrupted when he was drafted to serve in the army during the Franco-Prussian War (1870–71). Profoundly affected by the horrors he witnessed during his short time in the military, Redon settled back in Paris after the war with a new outlook. The death of his father shortly thereafter brought further emotional turmoil but also greater financial independence afforded by his inheritance. A small pen study in graphite and ink shows the attic apartment at 81 boulevard du Montparnasse that served as his residence and studio starting in 1874 (fig. 3). From this new home, after years of personal trials and false starts, Redon at last began to craft his distinctive view of the world through art.

During the 1870s and '80s, Redon established a signature visual language through what he called his *noirs*, drawings made in charcoal and other black media that had correspondingly dark subject matter. Built up from layers of dark pigment, the eerie compositions of drawings like *Cauldron of the Sorceress* (fig. 4) and *Apparition* (plate 1) eschew clear narratives in favor of haunting atmosphere and symbolism. Redon

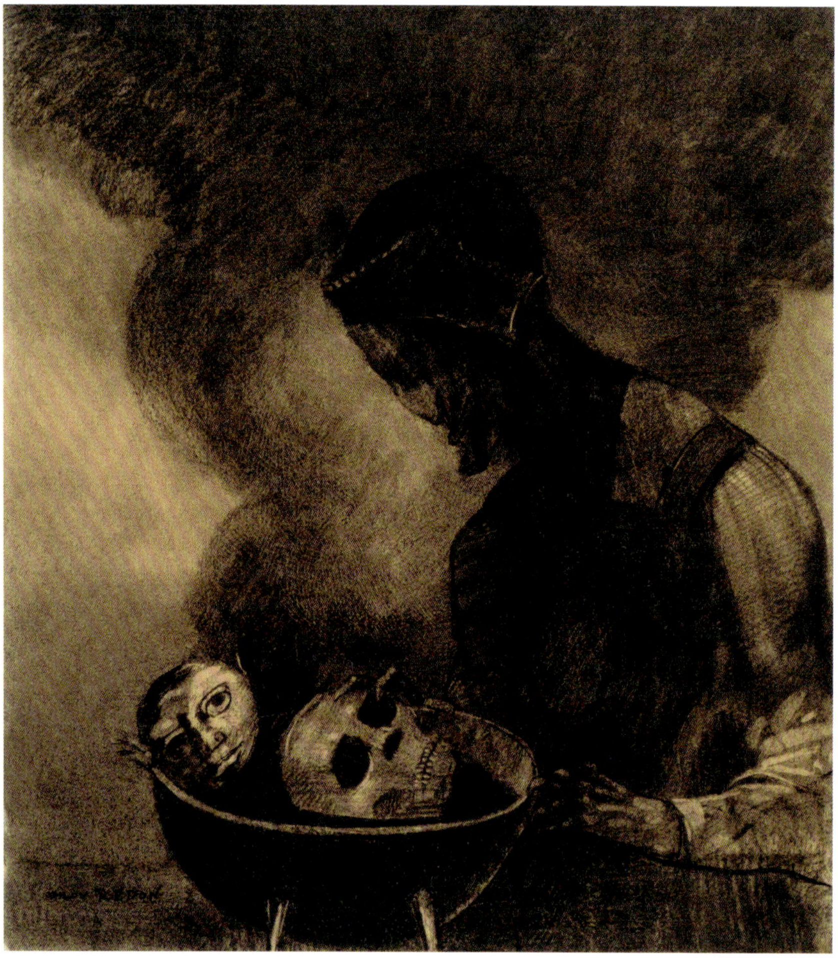

FIG. 4 Odilon Redon, *Cauldron of the Sorceress*, 1879. Various charcoals with stumping, erasing, and incising on pale-pink paper with red and blue fibers altered to a golden tone, 40.8 × 37.1 cm (16 1/16 × 14 5/8 in.). Art Institute of Chicago, David Adler Collection, 1950.1432

also began working in lithography, initially employing the medium to reproduce and further disseminate his monochromatic drawings before realizing the independent expressive capacity of printmaking. In 1879 he published *In the Dream* (*Dans le rêve*), the first of his eleven portfolios of lithographs, which featured several of his now characteristic surreal motifs, including severed heads, floating eyeballs, and shadowy barren landscapes (figs. 5, 6).

Redon preferred not to explain the meaning behind his surreal compositions. He defended this uncertainty as inherent to his art, stating, "The designation by a title given to my drawings is sometimes superfluous, so to speak. The title is not justified unless it is vague, indeterminate and aspiring, even confusedly equivocal. My drawings *inspire* and do not define themselves. They determine nothing. They place us just as music does in the ambiguous world of the indeterminate."[4] Nonetheless, the strange blend of imagery in Redon's *noir* drawings and lithographs

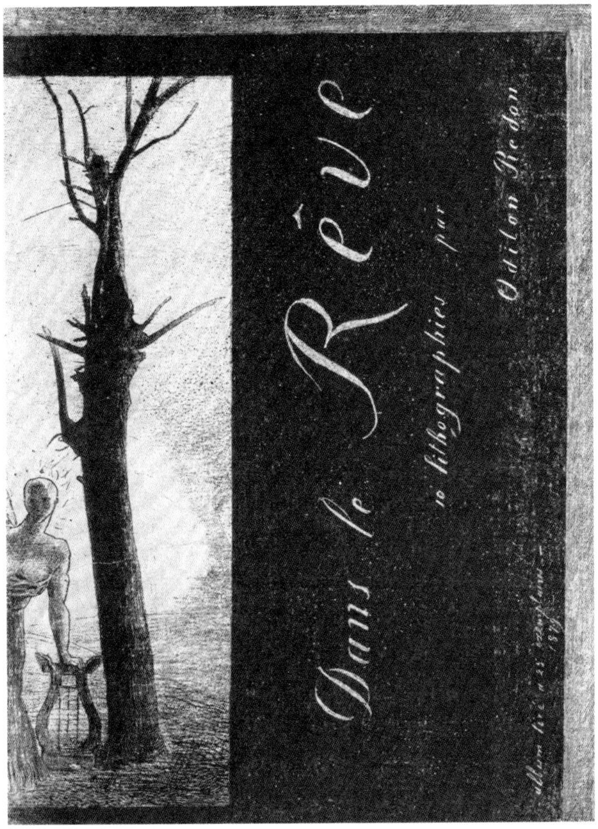

FIG. 5 Odilon Redon, Cover-frontispiece of the portfolio *In the Dream*, 1879. Lithograph, 53.4 × 36.9 cm (21 × 14 ½ in.). New York, Museum of Modern Art, The Sue and Edgar Wachenheim III Endowment, 293.2015.1

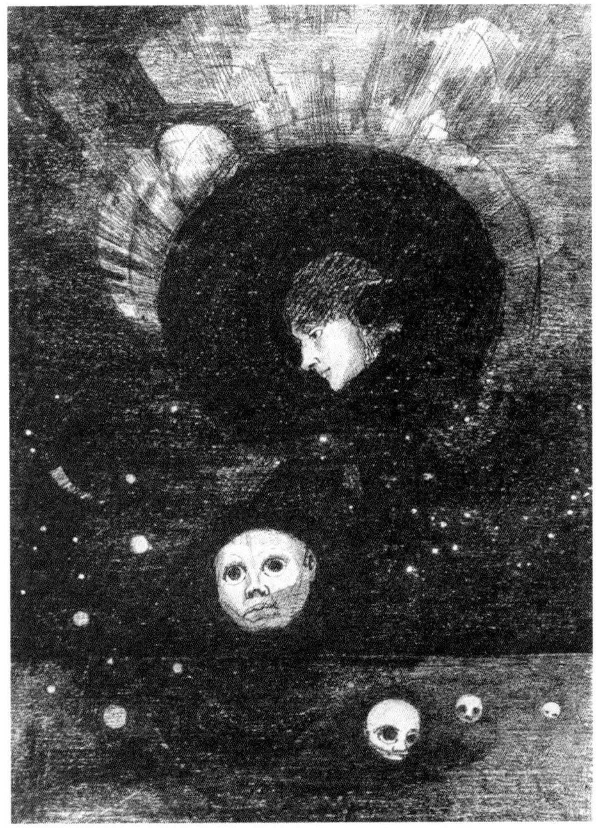

FIG. 6 Odilon Redon, *Germination*, 1879. From the portfolio *In the Dream*. Lithograph on chine appliqué, 53.2 × 37 cm (20 15/16 × 14 9/16 in.). New York, Museum of Modern Art, The Sue and Edgar Wachenheim III Endowment, 293.2015.2

along with their titles often offers insight into his diverse influences as well as his interest in the aesthetic and scientific developments of his time. The sea of small floating heads spread throughout the darkness in *Germination* (see fig. 6), for example, at first appears as mysterious and absurd as any of his other dreamscapes. Yet when combined with the title, a nod to Redon's fascination with modern plant science, the composition evokes the scattering of seeds or perhaps microbial forms as viewed through a microscope.

While Redon was resistant to labels, he was most closely aligned with Symbolism, an artistic and literary movement in the late nineteenth century that favored the dreamlike and subjective over the conventions of naturalism. Symbolist artists such as Gustave Moreau and Eugène Carrière often worked independently and were not united by a shared style or aesthetic goals. Instead, rejecting the direct representation of nature that was foundational to movements like Impressionism and

Realism, the Symbolists sought to express individual experience through a highly personal language of metaphor, color, and symbols. Redon found particular inspiration in the Symbolist poetry of Charles Baudelaire and Stéphane Mallarmé but was not limited by these associations. In the 1880s and '90s, he exhibited alongside varied groups of artists, including the Impressionists, the Nabis, and Les XX, without compromising his individual aesthetic.[5] Even with his commitment to independence, Redon was deeply immersed in the cultural landscape of Paris. He participated in literary salons, contributed prints to collaborative publications, and developed close relationships with collectors, dealers, and artists. In 1884 he was a founding member of the Société des Artistes Indépendants, an organization of artists—including the painters Georges Seurat and Paul Signac—that hosted an annual exhibition as an alternative to the official government-sponsored Salon.

Redon's immersion in the artistic milieu of Paris helped him to achieve greater renown, in part due to the publication of the Symbolist writer Joris-Karl Huysmans's 1884 novel *À rebours* (*Against Nature*), which features an eccentric and reclusive aristocrat who collects Redon's drawings. Huysmans's vivid prose captures the inimitable strangeness of the artist's subject matter:

> In their narrow gold-rimmed frames of unpainted pear-wood, they contained the most fantastic of visions: a Merovingian head balanced on a cup; a bearded man with something of the bonze about him and something of the typical speaker at public meetings, touching a colossal cannon-ball with one finger; a horrible spider with a human face lodged in the middle of its body. There were other drawings which plunged even deeper into the horrific realms of bad dreams and fevered visions. Here there was an enormous dice blinking a mournful eye; there, studies of bleak and arid landscapes, of burnt-up plains, of earth heaving and erupting into fiery clouds, into livid and stagnant skies. Sometimes Redon's subjects actually seemed to be borrowed from the nightmares of science, to go back to prehistoric times.... These drawings defied classification, most of them exceeding the bounds of pictorial art and creating a new type of fantasy, born of sickness and delirium.[6]

While many critics were scandalized by the decadence portrayed in the novel, it found popularity among a young generation of aesthetes and artists who grew interested in Redon's work.

Despite the critical and financial success of his shadowy, enigmatic compositions, around the turn of the century Redon unexpectedly transformed his art from an exploration of darkness to an expression of pure color. In 1899 he published *Apocalypse of Saint John* (plates 25–37), the last of his eleven black-and-white lithographic portfolios, which had served an important role in circulating his work to broader audiences. Now working primarily in oil paint and pastel, Redon retained much of the visual imagery and literary associations of his earlier career but also embraced new subject matter better suited to vibrant media, including floral still lifes and portraiture. Produced in bold color, these more conventional compositions allowed the artist to attain even greater commercial success while preserving his distinctive vision. Though contained in vases, the radiant flowers in his still lifes seem to emerge from the same dreamlike realm as his *noir* monsters, often appearing to float in the void of space (plates 42, 45) or in a nebulous field made of powdery pastel (fig. 7). He even experimented briefly with color lithography (plates 39, 40), finding inspiration in the contrast of bright hues in every part of his artistic practice. Redon's abandonment of black is often seen as a sharp break in his career, but, as this book demonstrates, the turn to color developed gradually out of the aesthetic and thematic concerns that were always central to his art.

§

Highlighting the extraordinary works by Redon in the collections of the J. Paul Getty Museum and the Getty Research Institute, the exhibition *Odilon Redon: Otherworldly Visions* and this accompanying publication aim to show the significance of the artist's lifelong practices of drawing and printmaking, and to introduce new audiences to his unusual subjects and technical innovation. The essays in this volume examine the chromatic evolution in Redon's oeuvre through these parallel artistic mediums. The first, "Darkness and Light: Redon in Charcoal and Pastel," delves into the artist's complex relationship to color in his drawings, from the multichromatic darkness of his charcoal *noirs* to the supernatural hues of his late pastels. It investigates the sophisticated range of media in Redon's *noir* works and his careful use of paper tone and fixative to provide elements of color in what seem at first glance to be monochromatic images. This study builds on the 2016 Getty exhibition *Noir: The*

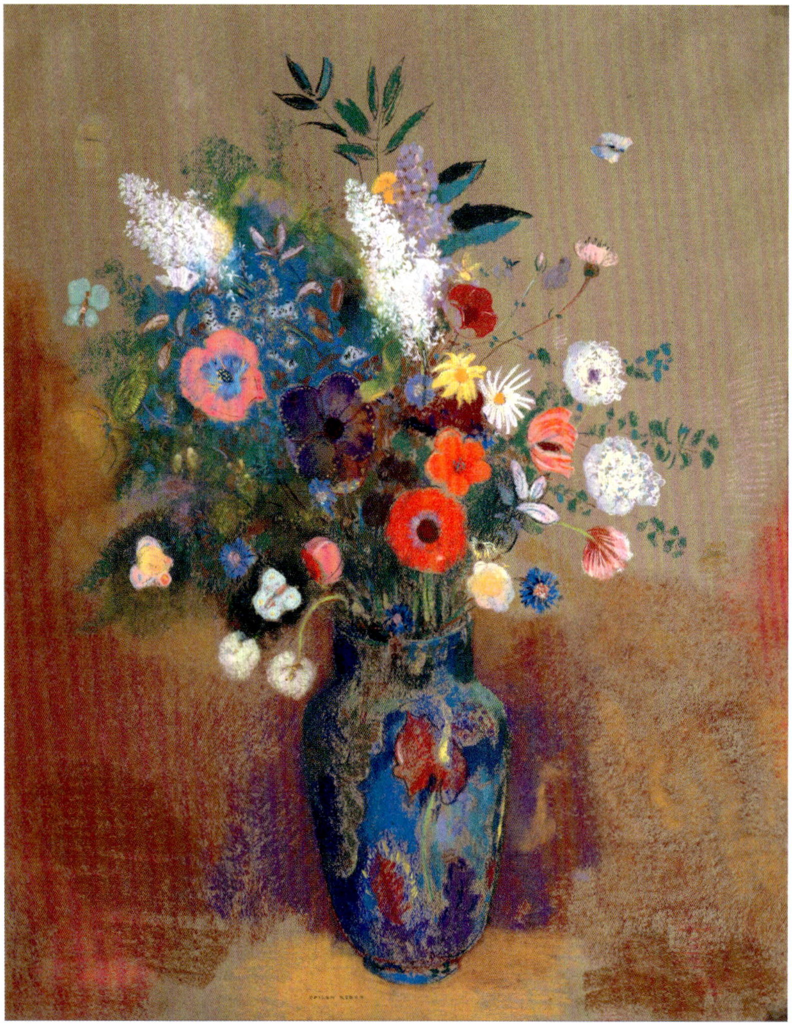

FIG. 7 Odilon Redon, *Bouquet of Flowers*, ca. 1900–1905. Pastel, 80.3 × 64.1 cm (31⅝ × 25¼ in.). New York, Metropolitan Museum of Art, Gift of Mrs. George B. Post, 1956, 56.50

Romance of Black in 19th-Century French Drawings and Prints, which provided foundational research on Redon's art in the Getty collection and its context within the broader use of black media in the nineteenth century.[7] The essay then explores Redon's shift to brightly colored pastel, highlighting his adoption of new subject matter alongside his reimaginings of compositions previously explored in black media.

The second essay, "Drawing on Stone: Redon's Lithographs," surveys Redon's career as a printmaker, illuminating the transformation of lithography in his work from a reproductive tool to an independent medium, and situating this change within the rise and appeal of lithography to artists in post-1850s Paris. The essay looks at Redon's interactions and relationships with printers and publishers, his brief engagement with color lithography, and ultimately his abandonment of the technique after 1900 as he dedicated himself more fully to the wild chromatic

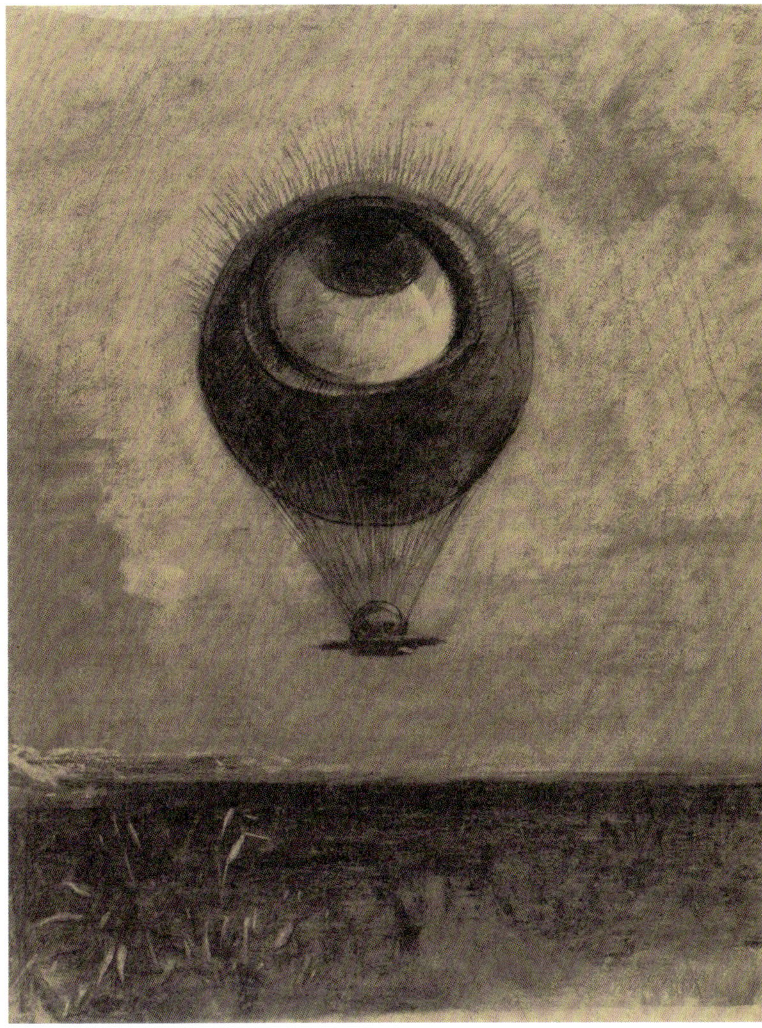

FIG. 8 Odilon Redon, *Eye-Balloon*, 1878. Charcoal and chalk on colored paper, 42.2 × 33.3 cm (16 5/8 × 13 1/8 in.). New York, Museum of Modern Art, Gift of Larry Aldrich, 4.1964

possibilities of color pastel and paint. Together these texts emphasize how Redon's experimental practices brought his spectral visions and macabre fantasies to life, and the resonances he found between drawing on paper and drawing on the lithographic stone. By considering Redon through his methods of production, this book focuses on the importance of technique in how the artist developed his fantastical compositions and the ways in which these processes persisted and sometimes shifted over time.

With its focus on materials and techniques, this project is an invitation to carefully observe the unusual world of Redon and the themes that endured throughout his career. For example, the artist maintained a preoccupation with the concept and representation of vision, which he explored in various mediums. In works like the drawing *Eye-Balloon* (fig. 8) and the lithograph *Everywhere Eyeballs Are Aflame* (plate 16), this fixation on sight was literalized in the depiction of disembodied eyes. Formed from

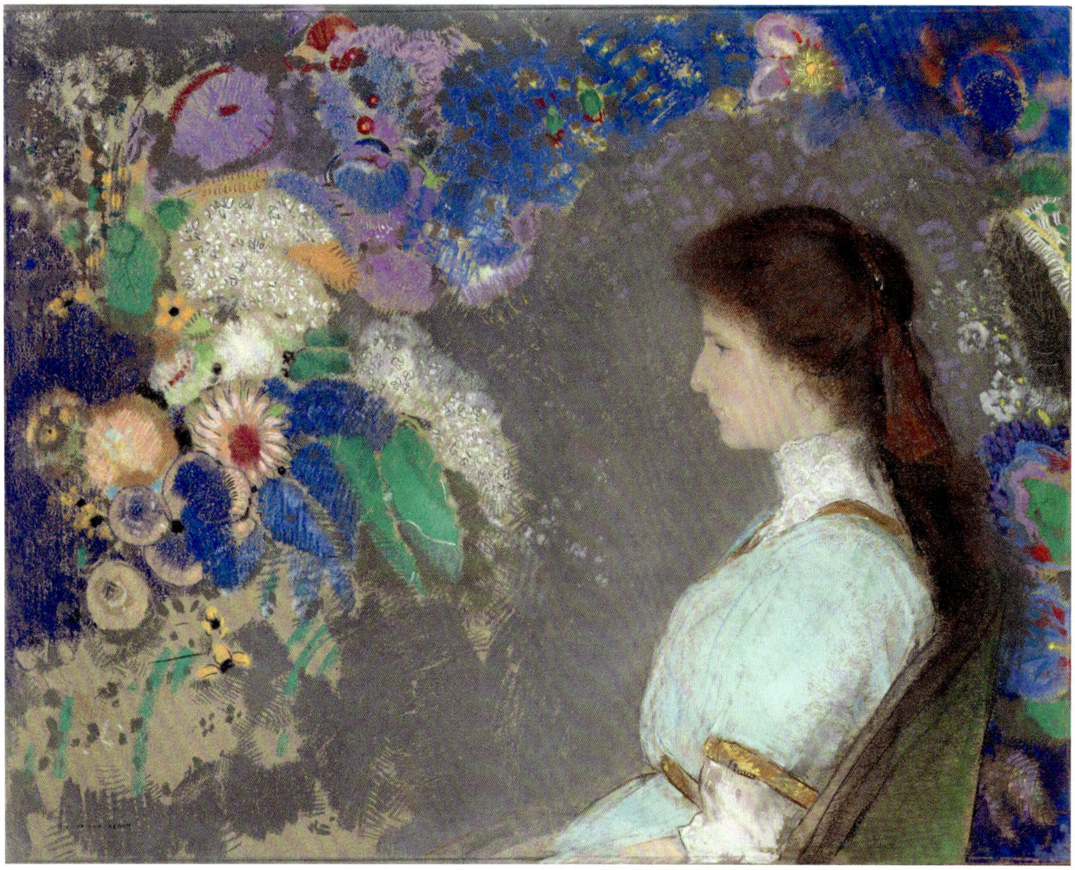

FIG. 9 Odilon Redon, *Violette Heymann*, 1910. Pastel on gray paper, 72 × 92 cm (28 ⅜ × 36 ¼ in.). Cleveland Museum of Art, Hinman B. Hurlbut Collection, 1926.1976

vaporous layers of charcoal or thick strokes of printer's ink, these eyeballs float freely in space, seemingly untethered from the earthly realm. As Jodi Hauptman describes them: "Let loose from the limitations of mind and body, Redon's eyes are free to *really* see, beyond reality, beyond nature, beyond the visible."[8] After transitioning to work in pastel, Redon found new ways to represent this otherworldly vision with striking color. The sitters in his portraits, like *Violette Heymann* (fig. 9) and *Baronne de Domecy* (plate 43), often seem to gaze out into the distance without seeing, appearing lost in reverie. Instead, the portraits depict a kind of spiritual vision, embodied in the explosion of radiant floral blooms formed around the figures, as if projecting their inner dreams.

With his hallucinatory compositions, Redon sought to similarly transport the viewer beyond the physical into the depths of imagination. In the lithograph *Light* (plate 5), he presents a voyeuristic depiction of this encounter with the surreal. Two small figures in the foreground stand in a dark room, looking up through an immense window at the brightly lit profile of a large, contemplative face. For viewers today, this work certainly evokes the experience of cinema, but here Redon also replicates the act of beholding his art, glimpsing the inexplicable as it is illuminated through a frame. *Odilon Redon: Otherworldly Visions* invites you to look closely at these strange and captivating works, to step beyond the frame and into Redon's imagination.

Notes

1 Redon 1986 [1922], 7. Much of what we know about Redon's life is dependent on *À soi-même, journal (1867–1915): Notes sur la vie, l'art et les artistes* [*To Myself: Notes on Life, Art, and Artists*], a compendium of letters, notes, and autobiographical statements published in 1922, six years after the artist's death, as well as biographies published by André Mellerio in 1913 and 1923, which reflect input from Redon and his wife, Camille. Redon was aware of his own role in shaping the perception of his life and art, so this information should be received with reservations. For more on the inconsistencies of Redon's personal biography, see Druick and Zegers 1994B.

2 Redon 1986 [1922], 10–11. Redon invited associations between his early life and his art in biographical statements throughout his career. For more on Redon's childhood and the mythology of its influence, see Druick and Zegers 1994B. These connections continue to inform Redon scholarship; see, for example, Stuffmann 2007, 15.

3 Delacroix originally conceived of *The Education of Achilles* as a part of a series of ceiling murals for the library of the Chambre des Députés but made several painted and drawn versions of the composition over his career, including the pastel shown in figure 2. Redon's drawn copy, now in a private collection, was made after a painted version exhibited in Bordeaux in 1863. He mentions his attachment to the copy he made in a letter to Andries Bonger dated January 17, 1901, reproduced in Redon 1923, 43–44. Redon wrote extensively about his admiration for Delacroix in a series of texts published in *Notes sur la vie* (Redon 1986 [1922], 140–52), including a discussion of an additional pencil study Delacroix made around 1845 of *The Education of Achilles*, now at the Louvre (MI 1079, recto).

4 Redon 1986 [1922], 22.

5 In 1886 Redon participated in the eighth and final Impressionist exhibition. His work appeared at the annual exhibition of the Brussels-based artists group Les XX in 1886, 1887, and 1890. In 1899 he showed several works with members of the Nabis in an exhibition at the Galerie Durand-Ruel in Paris that celebrated his influence on the group of younger artists.

6 Huysmans 1884, 84–85. English translation from Hauptman 2005, 13.

7 Hendrix 2016.

8 Hauptman 2005, 45.

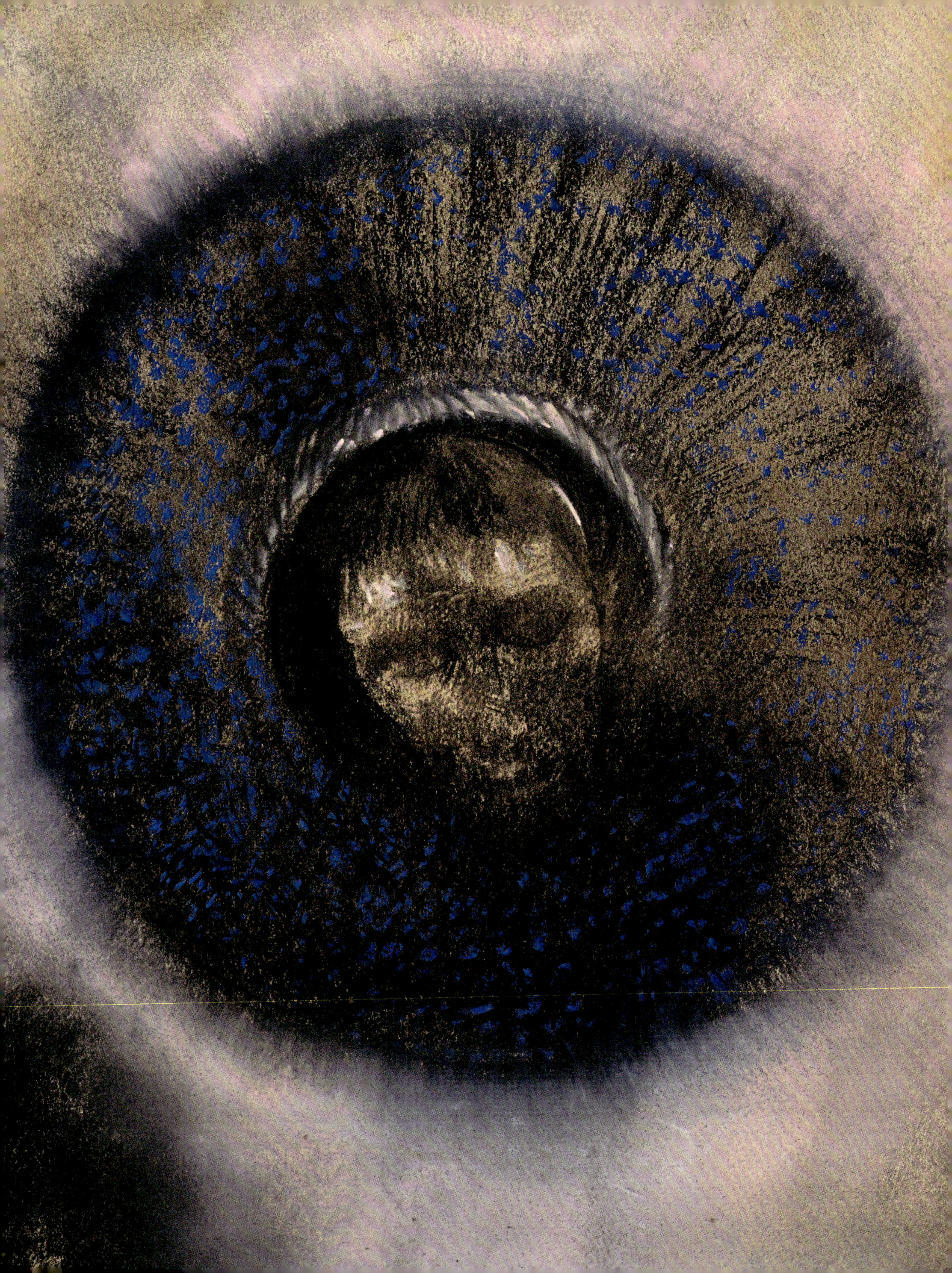

Darkness and Light: Redon in Charcoal and Pastel

Danielle Canter

The arc of Odilon Redon's career is often interpreted as being sharply divided by his transition from black media to the radiant hues of color pastel and oil paint. From 1870 to 1890, the artist focused primarily on creating what he called *noirs*, drawings made in charcoal and other black materials that explored equally tenebrous subject matter. From the rich darkness of the *noirs* emerged monstrous beasts and strange apparitions that were suited to his chosen medium. Shifting to work almost exclusively in color in the 1890s, Redon continued to explore the fantastical and surreal imagery that had characterized his *noirs* while incorporating new subjects better suited to bold hues. Yet it can be argued that his experimental pastels continued the ambitious approaches of his charcoal drawings, building on the dimensional and multichromatic compositions that he had achieved even while working within the limitations of black. Rather than a radical rejection of his earlier black works, the pastels illustrate Redon's sustained interest in technical innovation and the expressive potential of his materials. By examining the artist's early work in charcoal and, later, pastels, we can better understand the important role of drawing in expressing his personal vision.

For Redon the power of black was matched only by his boundless imagination. As he contended, "Black is the most essential color. . . . It is the agent of the spirit much more than the splendid color of the palette or of the prism."[1] The darkness in his works was multidimensional, built up from numerous shades of black pigment that allowed him to describe the enigmatic world of his dreams. Redon indeed saw black as a multichromatic color. He created complexity in his *noirs* through his choice of materials and working methods. The majority of his drawings were made in charcoal, a powdery medium formed from carbonized wood or vine twigs that was available in a range of dark grays and blacks. In the nineteenth century, newly manufactured variations of charcoal combined the material with different binders and additives to create a greater variety of hues, textures, and tonal values. The multiplicity of black media on the market allowed Redon and his contemporaries to depict the darkness of night and otherworldly shadows as never before, inspiring a wide array of fantastical subjects.[2]

Redon would often combine different forms of black media in his drawings for expressive effects. While charcoal was his primary medium, additional work in black chalk, conte crayon, and black pastels offered him a full palette of noir tones. This variety is visible in *Apparition* (plate 1), in which a bearded figure emerges from a dark void crafted from strong black marks. Even to the bare eye, multiple distinctive shades of black are discernible in the dense and atmospheric composition (fig. 10). A recent technical study of *Apparition* revealed that Redon combined six distinct materials throughout the drawing, including black and dark brown charcoals, black chalk, and various shades of black pastel.[3] He also selectively applied yellow pastel in the face of the figure, mirroring the warm tonality of the brown paper support. The varied consistency and hues of the black media, along with the blank reserves of paper, add depth and dimension to the ethereal portrayal of a ghostly figure.

Redon's paper supports provided a significant element of color to his work long before he embraced colored pastels as his principal drawing medium. The soft hues of his papers contrasted sharply with the deep blacks of charcoal and chalk. The paper itself was an essential component in constructing Redon's visionary world, as he often employed reserves as part of the composition. This is done to striking effect in *The Battle of the Bones* (plate 2), a darkly comic scene of two skeletons in the aftermath of physical combat, their broken bones scattered across the foreground as they attempt to keep fighting. The unusual composition was inspired by Maurice Bouchor's 1880 poem of the same name, which tells the story of two men who kill each other in a duel over a lover and, after death and burial, return to her home to continue the battle.[4] Set against an opaque black background, the wounded skeletons in the drawing are composed of blank areas of tan paper rather than the addition of media. With careful application of the thick charcoal and its selective removal, Redon fashioned the fine details of the skeletons from the bare sheet.

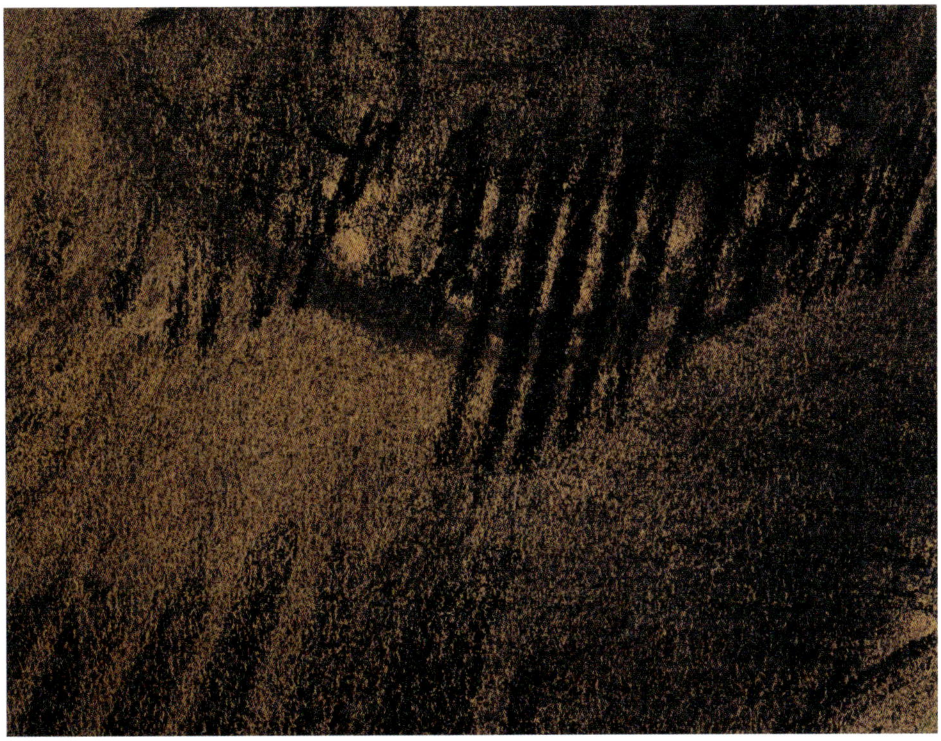

FIG. 10 Detail of the top center of *Apparition* (plate 1)

The relationship between paper tone and black media is also fundamental to the narrative of *The Tell-Tale Heart* (plate 3), one of four charcoal drawings Redon executed in 1883 related to the works of Edgar Allan Poe. Like many artists and writers associated with the Symbolist movement, Redon was inspired by the macabre imagery in Poe's stories.[5] These drawings, including *The Teeth* (fig. 11), are loosely interpretive of Poe's texts, building on the unusual imagery that was already central to Redon's oeuvre. *The Teeth* alludes to Poe's 1835 short story "Berenice," which tells of a man fixated on his fiancée, whose body is rapidly deteriorating from a debilitating disease. Redon, who already had a predilection for depicting disembodied body parts, captures the monomaniacal obsession of the narrator on the title character's teeth. In *The Tell-Tale Heart*, the artist similarly focuses on a singular anatomical subject. The ominous composition appears to elide several moments from Poe's famed 1843 short story of the same name.[6] The single eye floating in darkness at the center of the scene conjures the old man in the story, whose vulture-like eye haunts the narrator and eventually drives him to murder. The expanse of brown paper surrounding the dark abyss is made to resemble planks of wood, with Redon crafting striations and knots from minimal charcoal marks. Due to the horizontal line in the lower left of the drawing,

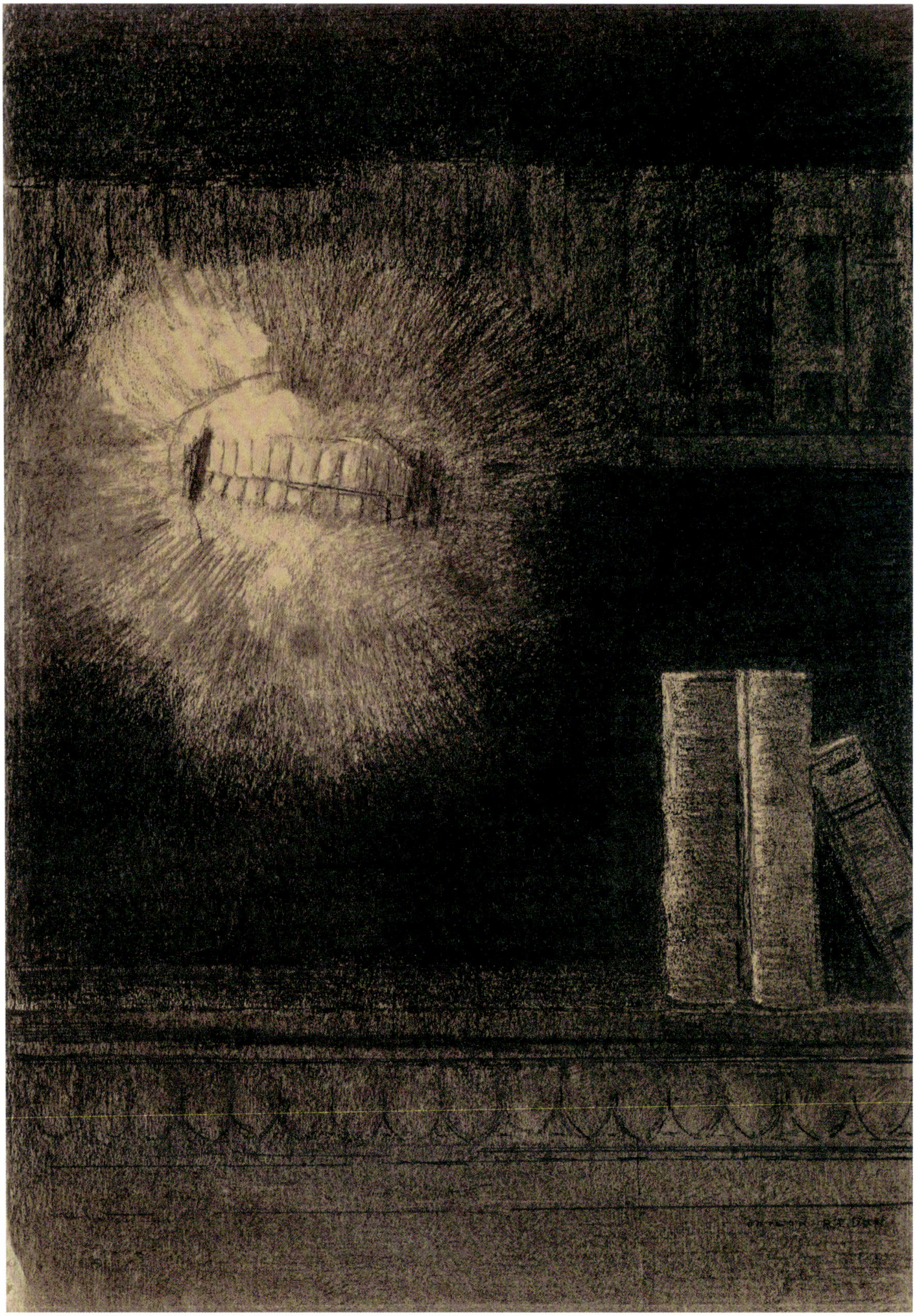

the wood appears more like the planks of a floor than those of a door. The drawing may also therefore refer to the end of the text, in which the narrator grows increasingly paranoid, believing he hears the heart of his victim beating under the floorboards, where he placed the body. The wood-brown tone of the paper ground allowed Redon to craft a trompe l'oeil allusion that suggests both scenes in the story.

Redon was deliberate in his choice of materials and techniques to develop a multichromatic effect in his black drawings. He intended the *noirs* to have multiple tonalities, later recalling: "The charcoal drawings ... were always made on paper tinted with pink or yellow, sometimes blue, thus showing my tendency or premise for color in which I later found the utmost pleasure and which overwhelmed me with delight."[7] Along with the subtle colors of his papers, now often faded to tan, Redon infused his drawings with an overall golden tone through the application of fixative. Used to adhere the friable media to the support, Redon's preferred fixative was made from tree resin, which imparted a soft yellow hue.[8] Since he retained many of his drawings in his studio for decades, the artist was aware that this effect became more pronounced over time as the resin darkened with exposure to light.

The warmth imbued by Redon's application of fixative sets the *noirs* apart from the starker black-and-white palette of most of his lithographs. Instead, the finished drawings appear almost aged, allowing Redon to emulate the appearance of discolored varnish on paintings. His friend and biographer André Mellerio recognized the artist's intentional use of this aesthetic effect, commenting, "By means of a fixative, of his own mixture, he gives his drawings a general mellowness that is dully golden and equivalent to the overall patina that Rembrandt's paintings acquire with age."[9] In works like *Apparition*, Redon applied fixative generously and in stages throughout the creation of the drawing, making it possible to layer and keep distinct his various forms of powdery black media. The resinous material saturated the paper, providing a yellow glow that enhances the effect of supernatural light diffused throughout the composition. The addition of yellow pastel in the face of the spectral figure contributes to this warm tonality, presaging the lively hues of pastel Redon would embrace in the following decades.

In the 1890s Redon began to shift away from the rich blacks of his *noirs* toward radiant color achieved with pastel and oil paint. Just as

FIG. 11 Odilon Redon, *The Teeth*, 1883. Charcoal and chalk, 51.1 × 36.8 cm (20 ⅛ × 14 ½ in.). New York, Museum of Modern Art, Gift of The Ian Woodner Family Collection, 284.2000

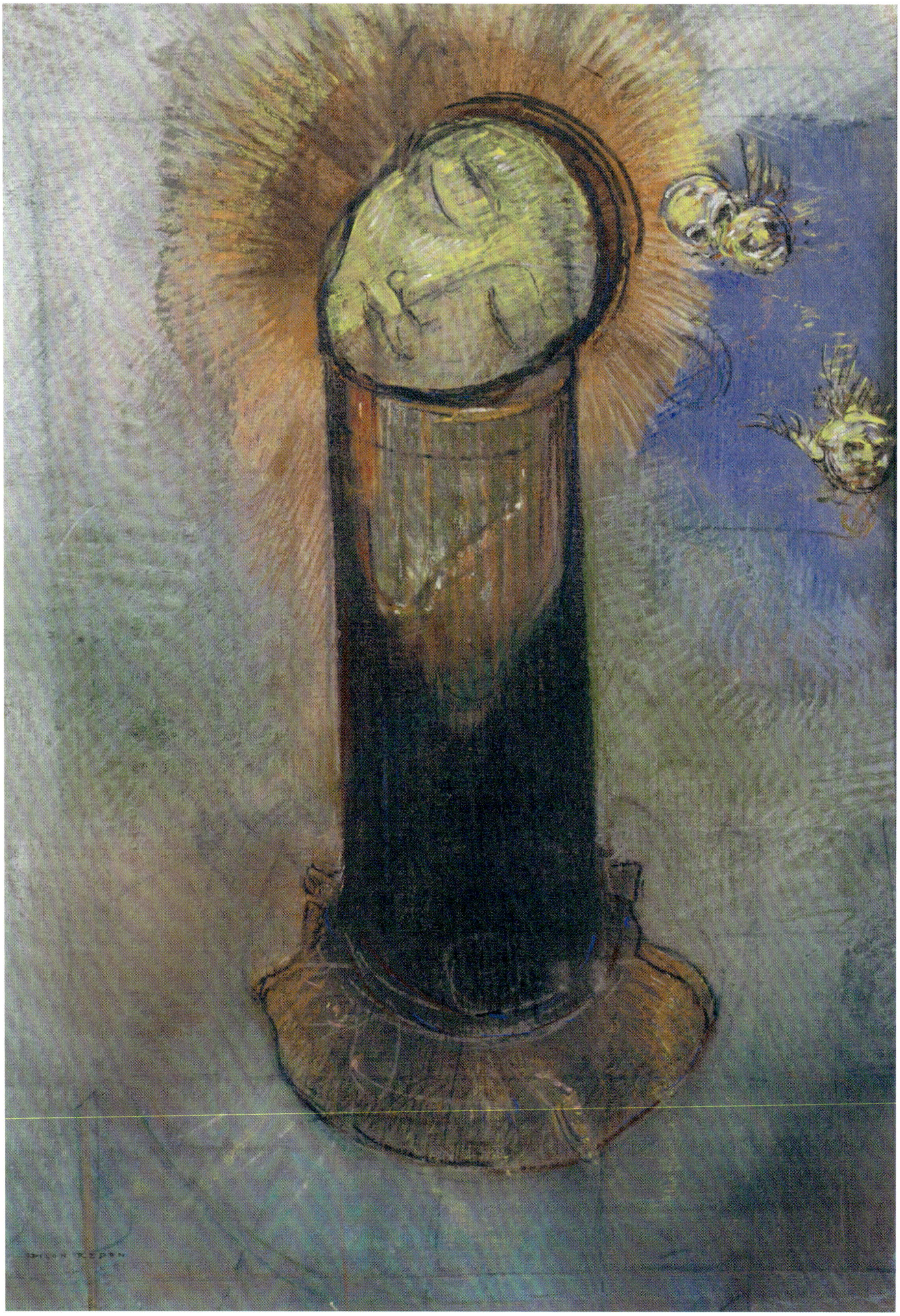

with his devotion to haunting and dreamlike subjects early in his career, Redon's unexpected transition to color has been associated with elements of his biography, as if he were emerging from a psychological darkness. His change in outlook has been attributed to the birth of his son Ari in 1888, after the death of his first son, Jean, in infancy in 1886, and to his improved critical and financial success as an artist.[10] His increasing involvement in group exhibitions as well as the popularity of Joris-Karl Huysmans's 1884 novel *À rebours* (*Against Nature*), which features an aristocratic collector of Redon's drawings, brought new attention to his work. Whether or not these changes in his personal life and career influenced his shifting relationship to his traditionally dark subject matter, the exploration of color in his drawings, paintings, and even prints is reflective of Redon's lifelong interest in the expressive capacity of various mediums.

Head Within an Aureole (plate 38), which dates to about 1894–95, represents a transitional moment as Redon began to incorporate color pastel more prominently into his drawing practice. The severed head surrounded by a circular halo at the center of the composition is drawn in charcoal, over which Redon layered scattered specks of ultramarine blue and a hazy cloud of pale pink pastel. On close inspection, the glowing head appears to be resting on a pedestal or pillar, barely visible beneath the cloud of pink powder on the surface of the sheet. The charcoal drawing likely originated as a depiction of the head of Saint John the Baptist—a biblical subject Redon rendered in a similar manner in other compositions (fig. 12)—before he obscured it with the application of loose pastel.[11] The mysterious form may now be read as one of Redon's disembodied eyes, the bold blue iris suspended in an indistinct space. The colorful pastel adds to the overall auratic glow he achieved with fixative applied to the paper. The ambiguity of the subject is heightened by the combination of materials, as the figure floats within a nebulous cloud of powdery pastel.

Despite developing his artistic reputation with his black drawings and lithographs, Redon had never fully rejected color media. He selectively employed color paint throughout the early decades of his career, most notably in light-filled oil studies of nature made near his childhood home (fig. 13). He also consistently incorporated color pastel and watercolor into his charcoal drawings to create subtle tonal effects, as he did for *Apparition*. The timeline for his transition to color is difficult

FIG. 12 Odilon Redon, *The Head of John the Baptist, on a Pillar*, ca. 1890. Pastel, 50 × 36.7 cm (19 11/16 × 14 7/16 in.). Amsterdam, Rijksmuseum, RP-T-1952-397

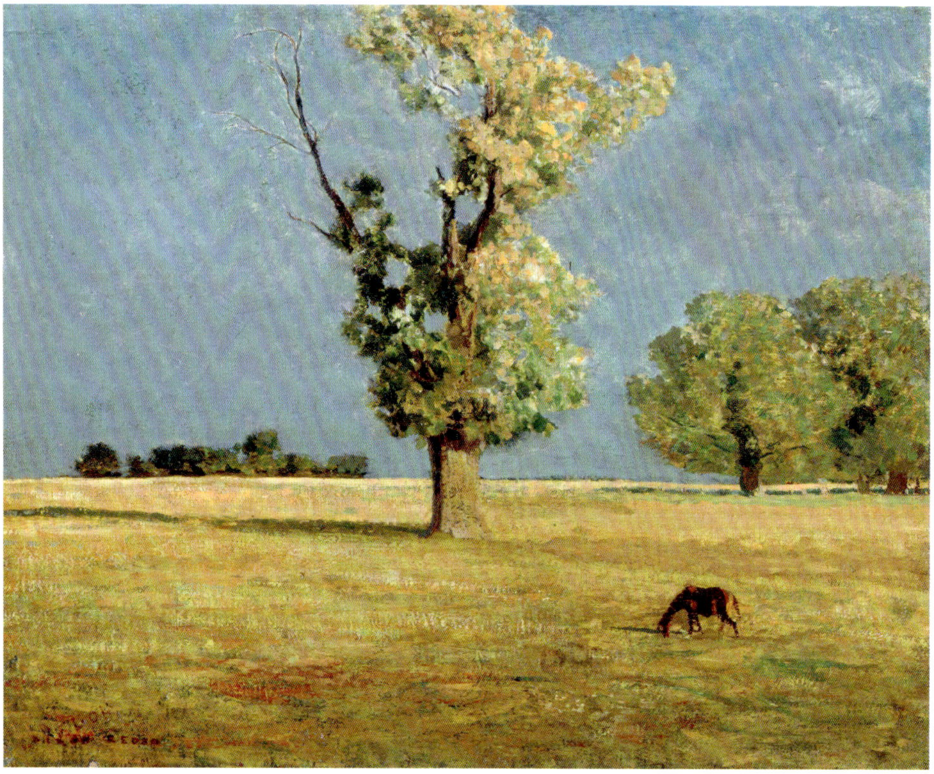

FIG. 13 Odilon Redon, *Médoc, The Tree*, ca. 1868. Oil on canvas, mounted on cardboard, 33 × 41 cm (13 × 16 ⅛ in.). Paris, Musée d'Orsay, Bequest of Mrs. Arï Redon in execution of the wishes of her husband, son of Odilon Redon, 1982, RF 1984 70

to determine, as Redon was known to rework many of his drawings at a later date. By the mid-1890s, however, it is clear that Redon no longer saw black media as the most effective means of expressing his singular vision.

Around the turn of the century, Redon fully abandoned his signature *noir* aesthetic, working almost exclusively in pastel and oil paint for the rest of his career. In color he continued to explore much of the surreal and dreamlike imagery that had characterized his black drawings and lithographs. The embrace of color media also brought new opportunities for technical experimentation in drawing, painting, and printmaking. The fine particles of pastel, for instance, could be manipulated and combined on paper in ways similar to charcoal. Redon was attuned to the particularities of each, stating, "A truly sensitive artist does not find the same invention in different materials, because he is affected by them differently."[12]

His consideration of material specificity is most evident when he applies the distinct expressive power of color pastel to subjects he had previously depicted in black media. Around 1881 Redon created *Head of*

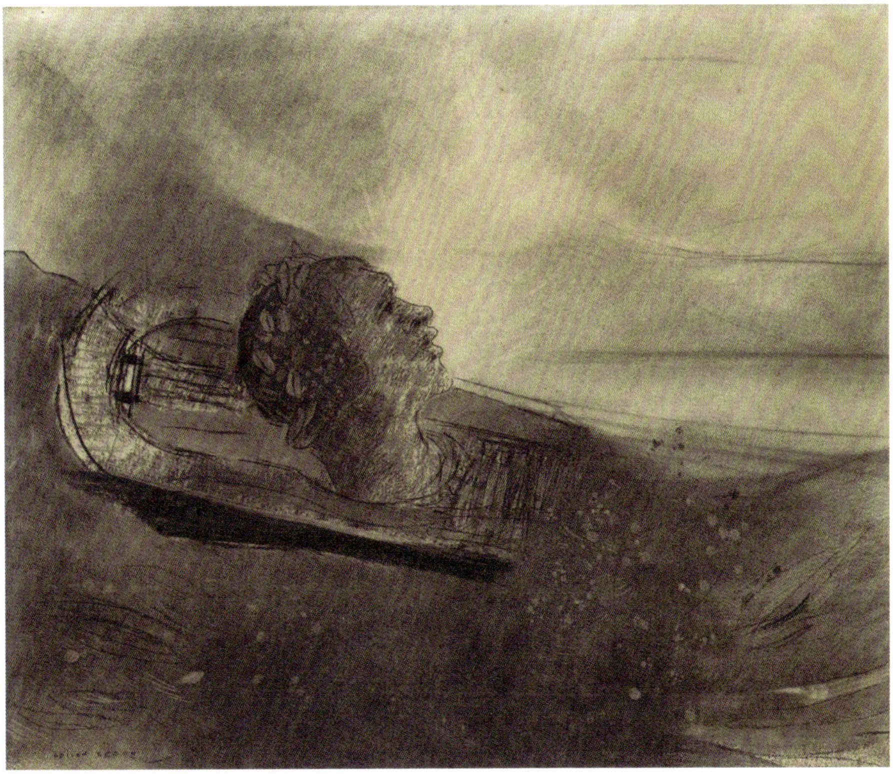

FIG. 14 Odilon Redon, *Head of Orpheus*, ca. 1881. Charcoal on colored paper, 44.5 × 53.7 cm (17 ½ × 21 ⅛ in.). New York, Museum of Modern Art, Gift of The Ian Woodner Family Collection, 285.2000

Orpheus (fig. 14), one of numerous representations he made of the mythic poet and musician.[13] Produced entirely in charcoal, the atmospheric drawing shows Orpheus's disembodied head resting on his lyre, suspended over dark waters. According to Greek myth, after death the tragic hero's head floated into the sea, still singing mournful songs. Rough lines and soft areas of powdered charcoal suggest mountains in the distance and a scattering of gray leaves over the water. When Redon returned to the subject in pastel around 1905 with a similar composition, he exploited the expanded palette to transform the scene. In *Orpheus* (plate 44), the suspended head of the poet is rendered through a simple outline on the bare gray paper. Crowned with a laurel wreath crafted from orange and yellow pastel, his ghostly presence is nearly lost within the abstracted white clouds that fill the bold blue sky. In pastel Redon brought new attention to the surrounding landscape, suspending Orpheus's head above a field of flowers exploding with pure color.

Redon had an enduring interest in depicting the natural world, and his transition to color inspired a particular dedication to the

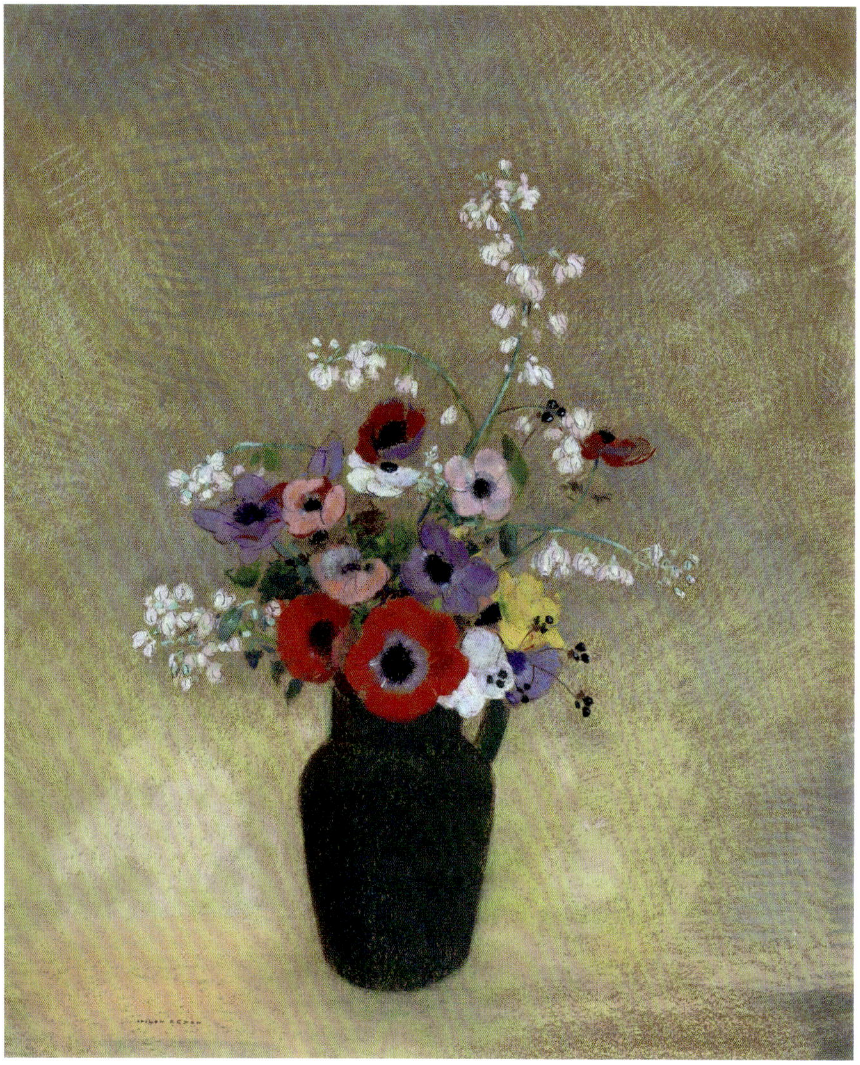

FIG. 15 Odilon Redon, *Large Green Vase with Mixed Flowers*, 1910–12. Pastel, 74.3 × 62.2 cm (29 ¼ × 24 ½ in.). Museum of Fine Arts, Boston, Bequest of John T. Spaulding, 48.591

representation of flowers and plants. Beginning in the 1890s, he produced hundreds of floral still lifes in pastel, often depicting blooms he cut in his own garden.[14] The compositions followed a model, as seen in *Vase of Flowers* (plate 42), consisting of a single vase or ceramic vessel filled with a radiant bouquet of blooms. As when he began making lithographs, Redon was aware of the marketability of this turn toward color and more seemingly conventional subject matter (see also "Drawing on Stone: Redon's Lithographs" in this volume). In 1900 he wrote to a friend about the success of this new pursuit: "I am working as always with great joy on my pastels. And they are pleasing, people want them, and they take them from me as soon as they are made."[15] Despite their broader public appeal, the flower studies reflect Redon's persistent affinity for playing with form and space. At times he included a suggestion of a table or other surface,

FIG. 16 Odilon Redon, *Madame Redon Embroidering*, 1880. Pastel over charcoal, 58 × 42 cm (22 13/16 × 16 9/16 in.). Paris, Musée d'Orsay, Bequest of Mrs. Arï Redon in execution of the wishes of her husband, son of Odilon Redon, 1982, RF 40490

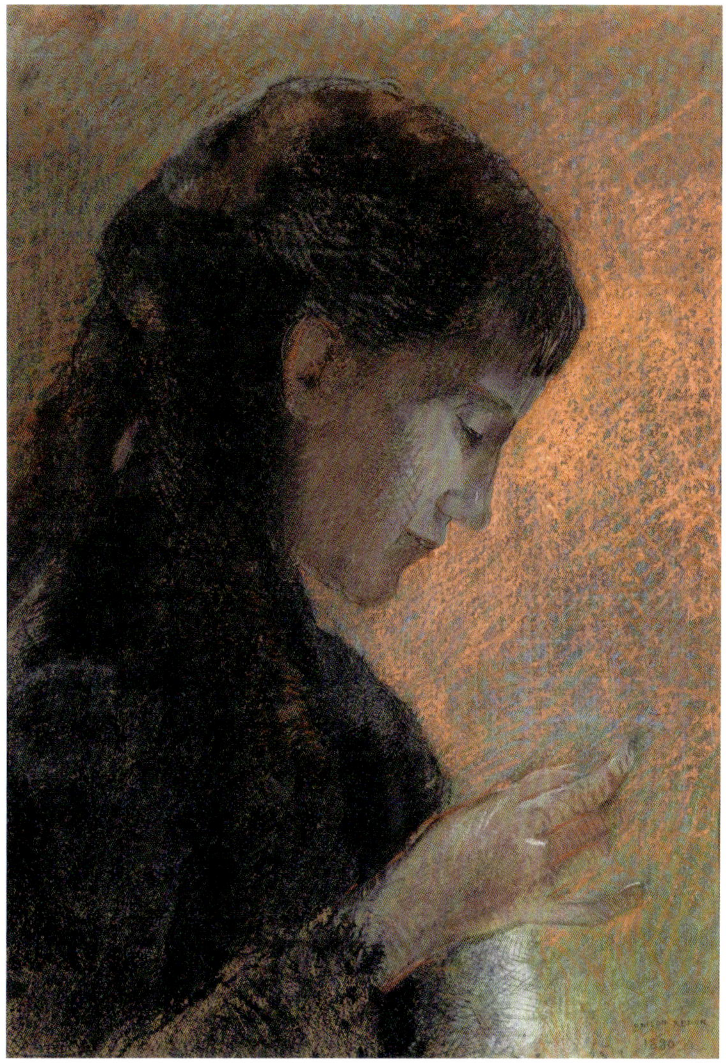

but the vases often appear to hover in an unidentifiable field (fig. 15), like the nebulous settings of his more enigmatic *noirs*. Though the works are grounded in direct observation of nature, the bold colors and spatial ambiguity in the flower studies express his singular artistic imagination.

Redon's pastel flowers figured prominently beyond the confines of vases and pots, often scattered across the background of his dreamlike portraits. The artist had been making intimate portraits of friends and family members throughout his career, including several studies of his wife, Camille (fig. 16), and son Ari. However, portraiture did not become central to Redon's work until he fully embraced color in the 1890s and began receiving commissions from patrons. An early example is his 1900 portrait of the Baronne de Domecy, née Cécile-Jeanne-Marie Frotier de Bagneux (plate 43), the wife of his friend and patron Baron Robert de

Domecy, made shortly after Redon had completed an ambitious cycle of decorative paintings for the couple's château in Burgundy. The baroness is shown in profile and appears lost in reverie, gazing out as if at a remove from the material world. Redon once again utilized the reserve of the paper, outlining the sitter's face and hair in graphite and black chalk on the tan ground of the sheet. Her monochromatic appearance contrasts sharply with her bright blue and red clothing and the radiant field of flowers that frames the composition. Neither entirely stylized nor precisely defined, the almost otherworldly flora seems to emanate from the figure, as if reflecting her inner visions.

Redon became increasingly ambitious and technically adept in his handling of color media after 1900. In this period, pastel sticks were available in a seemingly endless variety of hues and various hardnesses, which could attain different effects. Redon would often manipulate the media, wetting the ends of the sticks or brushing and stumping the pastel to blend and soften the colors on the surface of the paper, as seen in the feathery petals of the flowers surrounding the Baronne de Domecy (fig. 17).[16] He also incorporated strokes of graphite and chalk to outline figures and accentuate delicate details. Just as he did in his *noirs*, Redon adhered the powdery media to the support with fixative, incorporating it between applications of pastel to create a thick, layered effect. In order to avoid the overall discoloration seen in his charcoal drawings, however, he would frequently apply less fixative or not fix the top layer of his pastels to preserve the velvety surface and vivid color.[17]

As Redon achieved greater mastery of pastel, his depictions of the natural world became increasingly decorative and abstract. The flowers that bloom in the foreground of *Orpheus* more closely resemble fireworks than flora, formed from pulsing lines of pure color that defy anatomical structure (fig. 18). In 1905 a critic described Redon as "a painter of flowers as we see them in dreams. They do not bloom under the gardener's watering can in the rays of the sun. Their middays, made of moonlight and water from desecrated springs, give them the strength to live. They come from our nightmares and from oriental legends."[18] *Vase of Flowers—Large Composition* (plate 45), an enigmatic pastel made near the end of his life, features a female figure in profile gazing toward a vibrantly colored vase at the center of the sheet. While green fronds emerge from the mouth of the vessel, the surrounding space also teems with flowers and amorphous blooms of color with no clear source. On close inspection, the figure appears to be holding a rounded platter, largely concealed by the vase and ornate flora. Along with the woman's decorative armband, the presence of the platter suggests the pastel may have originally depicted the biblical figure Salome, whom Redon frequently represented holding

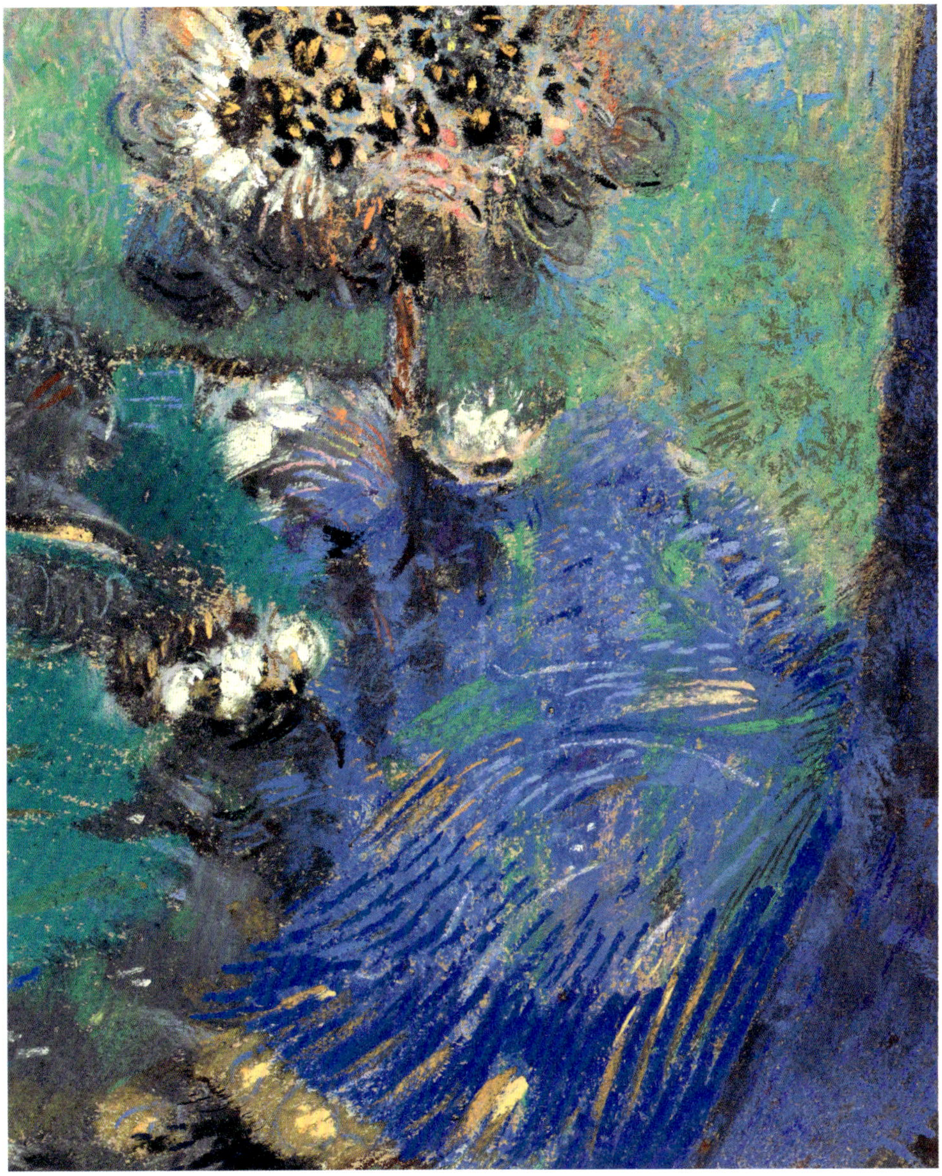

FIG. 17 Detail of the bottom center of *Baronne de Domecy* (plate 43)

the decapitated head of John the Baptist on a dish. By adding the oversize vessel to the center of the composition, the artist obscured this narrative, perhaps seeking to appeal to collectors who preferred his more decorative pastels. Although the drawing conforms to some extent to Redon's established template for floral still lifes, the dreamlike ambiguity of the composition evokes the more surreal qualities of his early *noirs*.

Rather than a radical divide, Redon's transition from darkness to light and color highlights the persistent thematic and aesthetic concerns that define his oeuvre and his particular affinity for drawing.

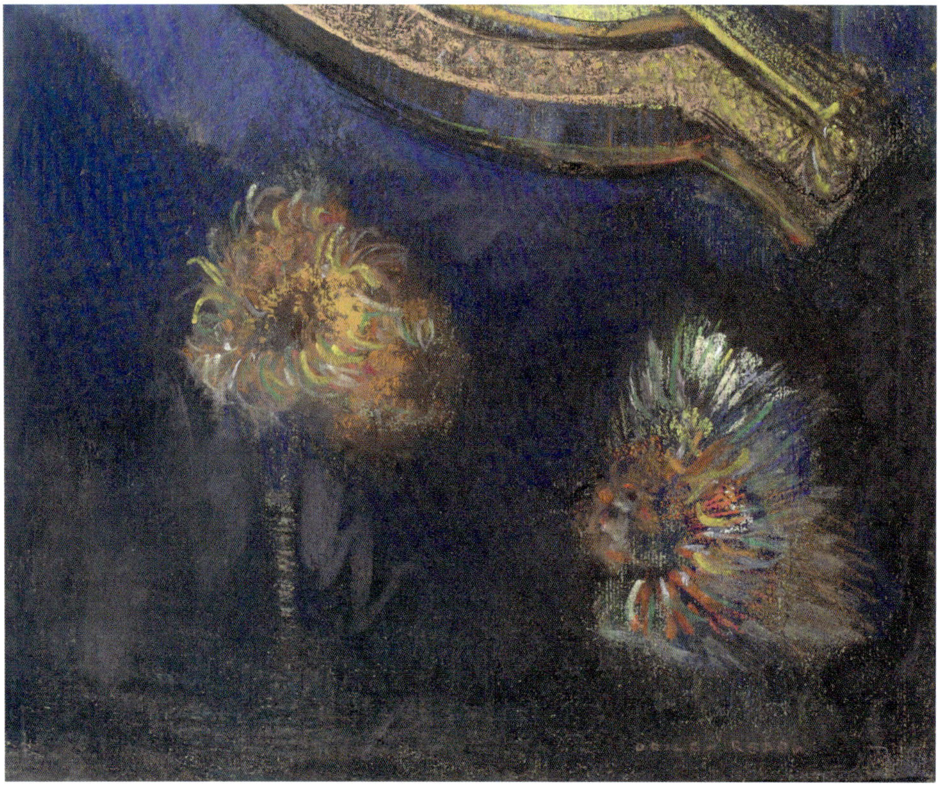

FIG. 18 Detail of the bottom right of *Orpheus* (plate 44)

The *noirs* and pastels are united by Redon's skillful manipulation of media and attention to subtle gradations of texture and tone. Despite their differences, the works in charcoal and pastel demonstrate how Redon, with attention to the specificity of his materials, used drawing throughout his career to express the surreal and highly personal visions of his imagination.

Notes

Translations mine unless otherwise noted.

1 Redon 1986 [1922], 103. The quote is from a 1913 lecture Redon gave in Holland on the occasion of an exhibition of his works.

2 For further discussion of the rise of black media in nineteenth-century France, see Hendrix 2016.

3 Daly et al. 2019.

4 Bouchor 1880. For more on Redon's illustrations of the poem, see Gamboni, Houssais, and Pinchon 2022, 186–87.

5 Despite producing multiple projects related to Poe's writing, including a lithographic portfolio titled *To Edgar Allan Poe* (*À Edgar Poe*, 1882), Redon later sought to deny the author's influence on his work. In a July 21, 1898, letter to his friend and biographer André Mellerio, he wrote, "I had been advised many times to read the American poet [Poe], as a support for my own art. My advisers were mistaken, I feel; his stories have never been my bedtime reading." (La lecture du poëte américan m'avait été conseillée comme devant me donner un appui à mon art. On se trompait, je crois; ses contes ne sont pas mon livre de chevet.) In Redon 1923, 31.

6 Gamboni 2011, 111–19.

7 Redon 1986 [1922], 103.

8 For more on Redon's fixatives and their material composition, see Stratis 1994; and Stratis 1995.

9 "Par un fixatif, mixture à lui particulière, il donne à ses dessins un fondu général comme doré sourdement, équivalant à cette patine d'ensemble que prennent en vieillissant les peintures de Rembrandt." Mellerio 1913, 19. Redon himself wrote repeatedly about his admiration for Rembrandt's art and its representation of darkness. In *To Myself* (Redon 1986 [1922], 28), he wrote: "Rembrandt gave me ever new surprises in art. He is the great human factor in the infinity of our ecstasies. He has given moral life to shadow. He has created chiaroscuro, as Phidias created the line. And all the mystery that art allows is hereafter possible only by him."

10 Douglas W. Druick and Peter Kort Zegers attribute Redon's embrace of color and new subject matter in part to his "increased success, marriage, and fatherhood." See Druick and Zegers 1994A, 173.

11 Severed heads are a prevalent theme throughout Redon's art. For further discussion of this imagery, including Redon's personal identification with John the Baptist, see Druick and Zegers 1994C.

12 "Un artiste vraiment sensible ne trouve pas la même fiction dans des matières différentes, parce qu'il est par elles différentes impressionné." Odilon Redon to André Mellerio, August 16, 1898, in Redon 1923, 33.

13 On Orpheus and the artist, see Wildenstein 1992–98, 2:66–71; and Leeman 1994, 230.

14 An entire volume of Redon's catalogue raisonné is dedicated to his flower works and landscapes. See Wildenstein 1992–98, vol. 3.

15 "Je travaille toutefois avec une grande joie à mes pastels. Et ils plaisent, on les désire, on me les prend aussitôt qu'ils sont faits." Odilon Redon to Andries Bonger, January 3, 1900, in Redon 1987, 78.

16 Stratis 1994, 362.

17 Stratis 1994, 373.

18 "M. Odilon Redon est un peintre de fleurs comme on les voit en songe. Elles n'éclosent pas sois l'arrosoir du jardinier aux rayons du soleil. Leurs midis dont de clair de lune et l'eau des sources profanées leur a donné la force de vivre. Elles émergent à la foise de nos cauchemars et des légendes orientales." Flament 1905. Albert Flament's comment was made in his review of the 1905 Salon d'automne exhibition at the Grand Palais in Paris, where five of the ten works Redon exhibited had floral imagery (nos. 1308, 1313–16). See Paris 1905.

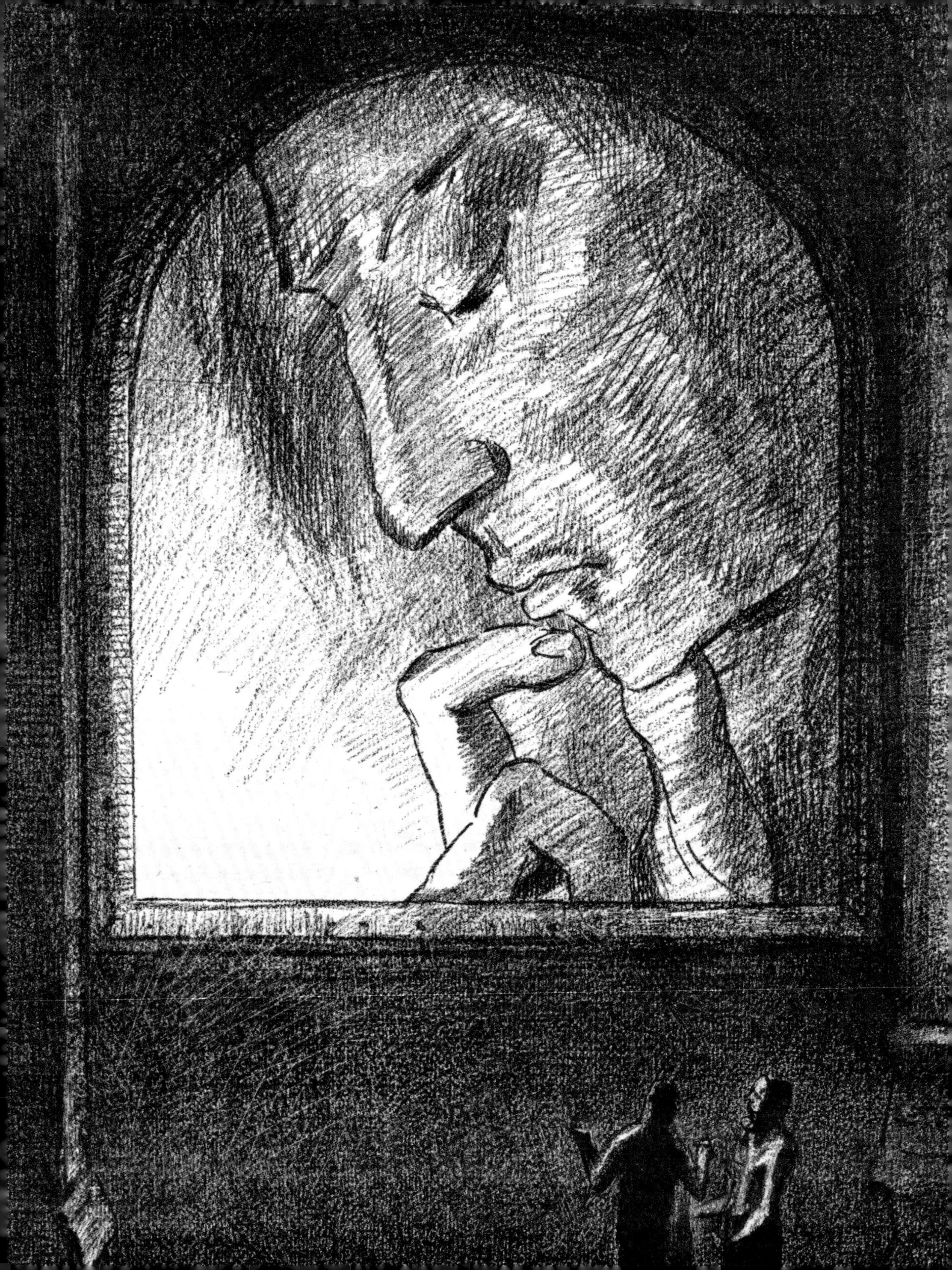

Drawing on Stone: Redon's Lithographs

Natalia Lauricella

In printmaking, Odilon Redon unearthed another rich channel through which to explore the dark recesses of his vivid imagination. Lithography especially intrigued the artist, who found a strong affinity between the print process and drawing. Over the course of two decades, Redon produced approximately 170 lithographs, working with a variety of publishers and master printers to push the boundaries of the medium even before critics and peers accepted it as a viable tool for original artistic expression. Between 1878 and 1896, Redon remained particularly committed to investigating the potentials of monochrome lithography. He played with the stark contrast of the black ink and white paper to convey fanciful and mysterious images, from floating eyeballs to grinning spiders. In addition to this extensive monochromatic work, he made a brief foray into color lithography. Indeed, with the medium's potential for reproduction as well as original production, lithography offered him a particularly fertile platform to further his aesthetic vision.

Redon encountered printmaking early in his artistic career. While living in his hometown of Bordeaux in the 1860s, he met Rodolphe Bresdin, a printmaker and draftsman who explored fantastical subjects and landscapes in his works on paper. Contemporary writers such as Charles Baudelaire and Joris-Karl Huysmans greatly admired Bresdin's work. One of his best-known prints is the 1861 monochrome lithograph *The Good Samaritan* (fig. 19), which Redon later described as the artist's attempt to "initiate us into the impressions of his own dream. A mystical and very strange dream."[1] Redon began to visit the artist's studio around 1865, and there he learned about complex and intricate line work from

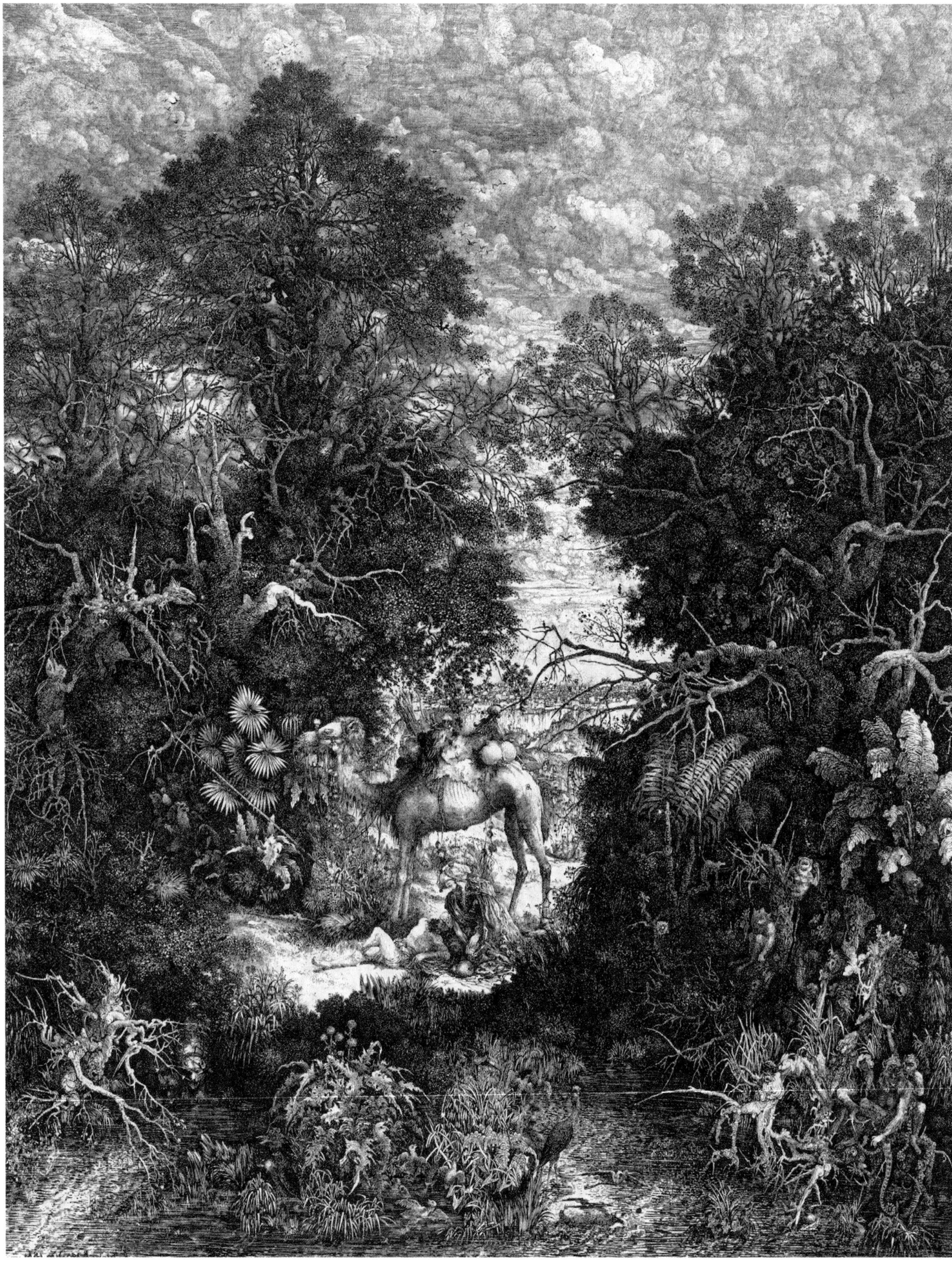

the woodcuts and engravings of Albrecht Dürer, and the mastery of chiaroscuro from the etchings of Rembrandt. Under Bresdin's tutelage, he tried his hand at etching and likely learned the techniques of lithography, though it was not until the late 1870s that Redon fully recognized lithography as a promising medium for constructing monochrome dream worlds.

Used for reproductive printing as well as original fine art production, lithography transformed the visual culture of the nineteenth century. Invented around 1796 by Alois Senefelder in Germany, lithography soon became a popular printmaking process, quickly appealing to printers in Europe because of its efficiency and the durability of the materials. The first lithographic printers in France established ateliers in Paris in the 1810s, and the simplicity and ease of the medium immediately intrigued painters who exhibited at the official Salon.[2] As a planographic process, lithography does not require the laborious work of carving wood or incising metal, as do the early print methods of woodcut and engraving. Based on the principle that water and oil resist each other, lithography is a chemical process involving a thick limestone block onto which an artist draws an image directly with an oil crayon. Without extensive training, artists can freely compose on the stone's surface, almost as if drawing on a piece of paper. A chemical mixture applied by a printer fixes the image on the stone's surface, which is then dampened with water that is repelled by the oil marks. When the printer applies an oil-based ink to the stone, it adheres only to the oil-crayon marks of the original drawing, which is then transferred to a sheet of paper when the stone passes through a printing press.

Visiting small lithographic print shops in Paris, painters such as Théodore Géricault, Antoine-Jean Gros, and Carle and Horace Vernet experimented in the young medium, exhibiting their monochrome lithographs at the Salon as early as 1817. Some artists, such as Anne-Louis Girodet, reproduced their paintings through lithography, whereas others, such as Géricault, Eugène Delacroix, and Honoré Daumier, considered lithography to be an experimental form of drawing and used the medium to produce original compositions.

The second half of the nineteenth century witnessed dramatic technological changes in lithography, particularly color lithographs, which became easier and faster to produce at a large scale due to

FIG. 19 Rodolphe Bresdin (French, 1822–1885), *The Good Samaritan*, 1861. Lithograph, 76.5 × 61.7 cm (30 ⅛ × 24 5/16 in.). Washington, DC, National Gallery of Art, Gift of David P. Becker, 2011.41.2

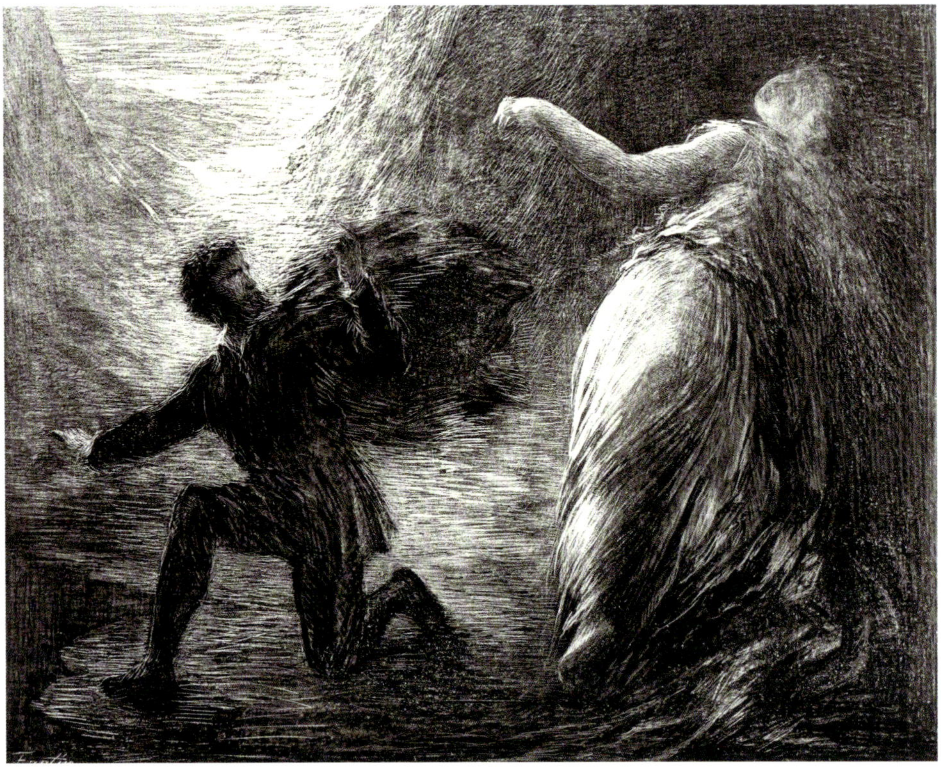

FIG. 20 Henri Fantin-Latour (French, 1836–1904), *Manfred et Astarte (Rob. Schumann, Manfred, no. 11)*, 1879. Lithograph, 40.3 × 51.3 cm (15⅞ × 20³⁄₁₆ in.). Fine Arts Museums of San Francisco, Achenbach Foundation for Graphic Arts, Gift of Theodore M. Lilienthal, 1959.122.11

advancements in the stone registration system and the introduction of steam presses.[3] The still-recognizable Belle Époque posters designed and printed by Jules Chéret popularized color lithography across commercial and fine art spheres beginning in the 1860s. Some artists, however, including Édouard Manet and Henri Fantin-Latour, continued to find monochrome lithography, with its deep black ink tones, appealing (fig. 20). Fantin-Latour took up lithography in the 1870s, exploring inventive techniques for drawing on stone, such as scraping and rubbing, and often working with the medium as a preparatory step in designing complex compositions for his oil paintings.[4]

With the encouragement of Fantin-Latour, whom he had befriended at a salon in Paris, Redon returned to lithography with a more serious focus around 1878. At this point in his career, Redon had not yet achieved critical acclaim, although he had been steadily developing a unique visual language and exploring enigmatic subjects through charcoal on paper (see fig. 8). Lithography was a logical choice for the artist, who saw it, like others had before him, as a process through which he could extend

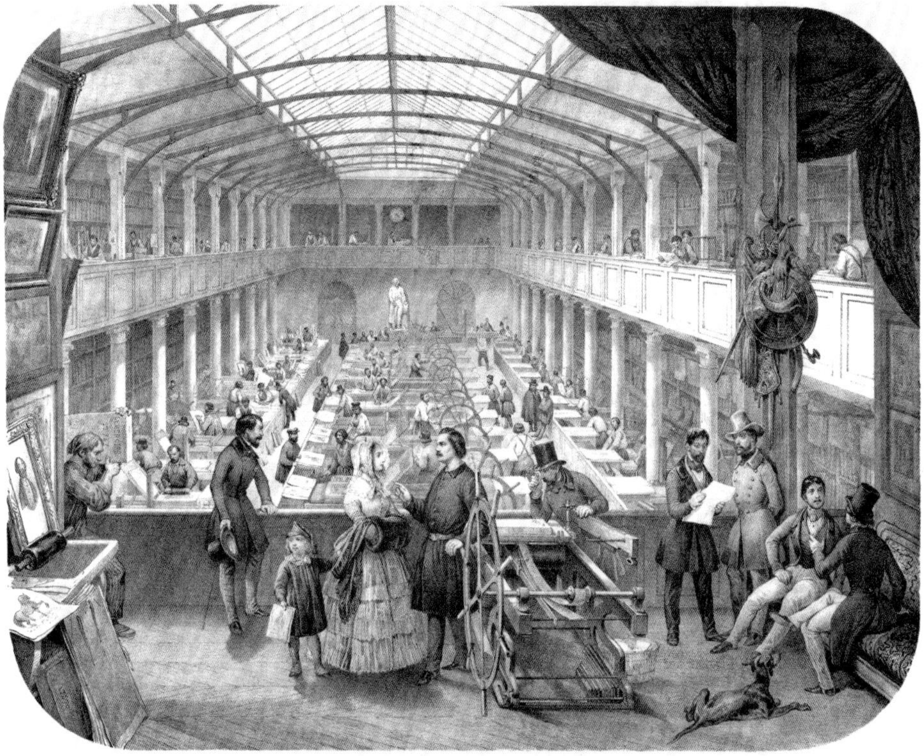

FIG. 21 Charles Villemin (French, act. 1835–49) after Victor Adam (French, 1801–1866), *Interior of Lemercier's Lithographic Printing House*, ca. 1846. Lithograph, 45.7 × 56.8 cm (18 × 22 ⅜ in.). New York, Metropolitan Museum of Art, Gift of E. Weyhe, 1923, 23.13

his work in drawing. Indeed, the craggy texture of the lithography crayon on stone translated into print the material effect of charcoal. Redon was intrigued by the reproductive potential of lithography: to multiply his drawings and circulate his singular aesthetic to a wider audience.

Redon's ability to engage so deeply in the lithographic process and to work so extensively in the medium was thanks to the involvement of professional printers who collaborated with the artist and undertook the complex technical aspects of printmaking. In his forays into lithography in the 1870s and '80s, Redon often worked with printers at Lemercier et Cie, the largest lithographic firm in Paris (fig. 21). Founded in 1828 by Rose-Joseph Lemercier, the firm was responsible for many important innovations in lithographic printing processes as well as the manufacture of lithographic materials, such as crayons.[5] Though Lemercier primarily produced commercial prints and advertising materials, the company also printed fine art lithographs, including both high-end reproductions and original art prints. Specially trained printers, such as Auguste Clot and Edouard Duchâtel, collaborated with artists to help them realize their work. It was in Lemercier's *ateliers artistiques* that Redon produced the contents of his portfolios *In the Dream* (*Dans le rêve*, 1879) and *The Origins* (*Les origines*, 1883). These early albums illustrate Redon's growing interest in the lithographic medium as he strove to develop a highly personal, Symbolist aesthetic. Through tonal contrast and soft, painterly textures, he created ethereal atmospheres from which arose ambiguous and imagined forms, like the phantasmal figures from *In the Dream* (see figs. 5, 6).

Perhaps with the guidance of printers, Redon used various lithographic materials and continued to develop techniques that enabled him to explore his visions in print.[6] He employed lithographic crayons, with which he would draw on transfer paper or directly on the limestone block surface. Lithographic crayons came in varying degrees of softness and hardness. With a hard crayon, Redon could produce a fine line; soft crayons allowed him to create areas of rich and velvety black. The tonal range of the lithographic crayon and its expressive versatility on the stone's surface offered Redon a means to materialize his dreamlike visions, in which strange creatures, figures, and objects often emerged out of dark shadows.

The 1887 print *Christ* (plate 4) demonstrates the range of marks that Redon achieved on the lithographic stone. For this close-up depiction of Christ's face, the artist played with the dramatic contrast of black ink and the white of the page to capture his subject's suffering. He applied numerous parallel lines to the stone with a hard crayon, using lighter pressure in some areas to convey the presence of light. Around the figure's face, the black marks become deeper and richer, an effect perhaps created through the application of soft crayon. From this blanket of black ink, Redon removed material using a scraper to characterize the jagged thorns of Christ's crown (fig. 22). He took full advantage of the generous tonal range of black and the strong contrast between dark and light to create an otherworldly and melancholic scene. It is possible that Redon worked on this particular print with Clot, who would go on to print the artist's portfolio *Temptation of Saint Anthony* (plates 7–17) as well as his two color lithographs.[7]

What especially appealed to the artist in his second foray into printmaking was the possibility for greater artistic freedom afforded through the use of transfer paper in the lithographic process, a practice that Fantin-Latour introduced to him in 1878. Though Redon had worked extensively on the stone, he famously detested the experience, finding the stone "cantankerous and peevish, like a capricious and nervous person," and vastly preferred to work in privacy, away from the hustle and bustle of a print atelier.[8] Transfer paper also made the process of producing a

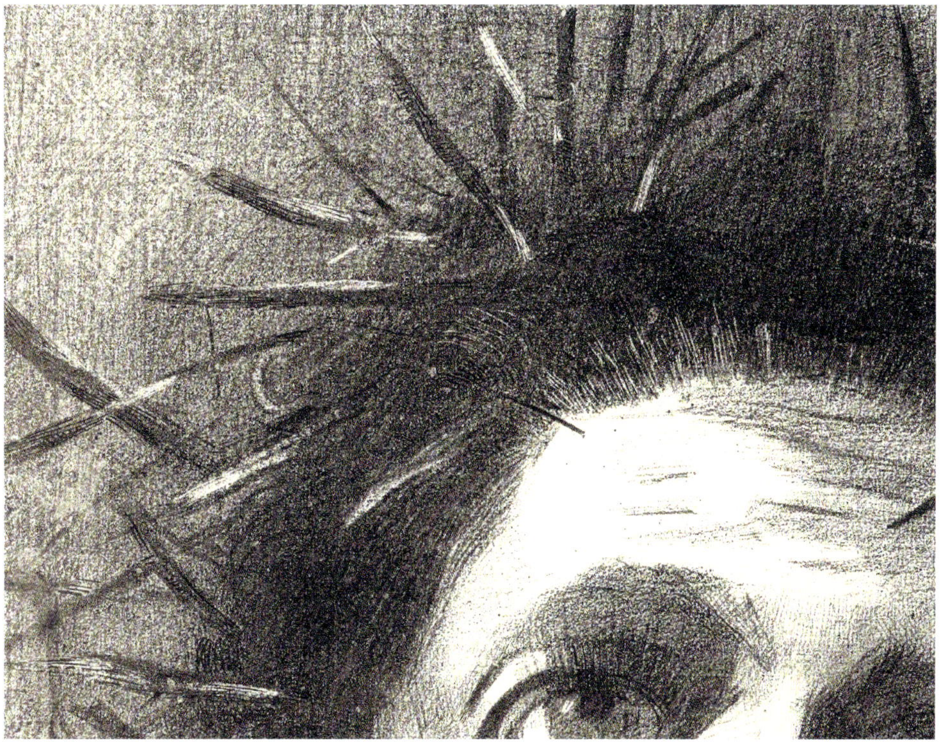

FIG. 22 Detail of the upper center of *Christ* (plate 4)

lithograph much easier, offering artists a familiar surface on which to translate their visions. In Redon's case, it was closely aligned with his practice of charcoal drawing.[9] Working on transfer paper also allowed for more flexibility in case of a mistake. Artists could simply discard a drawing rather than undergo the complex process of grinding away the area of the stone that held an error. After completing a drawing with lithographic crayon on paper, Redon handed it to a printer, who would transfer the drawing onto the stone's surface. Redon then finessed the composition directly on the stone before the printer pulled a proof for review.[10]

More pleased with this newly adopted method, Redon embarked on his extensive practice in lithography. He often worked in series, which allowed him to unfold a narrative over a group of prints within a single portfolio.[11] These albums were sold as complete editions, often in a designated order, within a specially crafted folder or box. His inspiration came largely from literary texts and biblical stories, such as his 1899 portfolio *Apocalypse of Saint John* (plates 25–37), which depicts Saint John's vision as narrated in the Book of Revelation. He also, over the course of nearly a decade, created three portfolios inspired by Gustave Flaubert's 1874 novel *La tentation de Saint Antoine* (*The Temptation of Saint Anthony*), which describes Saint Anthony's experience of being besieged by nightmarish visions while in the desert. Redon's first iteration, from 1888 (plates 7–17), was published by Edmond Deman in Brussels and printed by Becquet in Paris. Rather than literally illustrating Flaubert's text, Redon evoked the emotional and spiritual intensity of the story. He created eerie scenes in which strange entities—disembodied heads, floating eyeballs, and hybrid creatures—hover in undefined spaces, bright forms emerging from the dark depths of inky-black backgrounds to haunt Saint Anthony. The story and these apparitions continued to have a hold over the artist. A second series appeared a year later, in 1889, and the dealer Ambroise Vollard published Redon's final and longest album devoted to the novel in 1896.

Many of Redon's early prints were self-published, but by the 1890s he had created lithographs with some of the most important print publishers of the period, including Vollard, André Marty, and Gustave Pellet. Redon contributed *Old Knight* (plate 6) to Vollard's 1896 *The Album of Painter-Printmakers* (*L'album des peintres-graveurs*), a compilation of original prints by avant-garde artists, some of whom went on to become prominent figures in the history of art lithography. The print depicts a somber figure accompanied by fantastical creatures, executed in the artist's characteristic range of lithographic marks, from thin hatching in the upper left corner to the deep, rich black tones of the figure's garment. Redon also used the reserve of the print—the white of the paper where there is an absence of ink—to render the open window through which light streams, illuminating the room and the knight's contemplative expression.

It was around this period that Redon first introduced color into his printmaking. In 1897 he produced *Head of a Child with Flowers* (plate 39), published by Pellet, featuring a young figure in profile. The child's face is framed by curls rendered in brown tones that are further highlighted by marks made through scraping. Printed at Lemercier—and likely prepared by Duchâtel—in an edition of thirty-five in black ink, an additional fifteen impressions were printed in brown ink. The lighter impressions illustrate the artist's exploration of tonality through brown wash in what is an early experimentation with color. A rare impression printed in brown ink, now held at the Van Gogh Museum, has additions of light blue and yellow in the top right corner, hand applied in color pencil, likely by the artist (fig. 23). This print, with its subject's downturned profile, has a close compositional resemblance to one of the artist's color lithographs, *Beatrice* (plate 41), also made in 1897.

With *Beatrice*, a rendering of the Italian poet Dante Alighieri's muse, Redon moved fully into the realm of color lithography. Though color lithography had a strong association with commercial printing in the

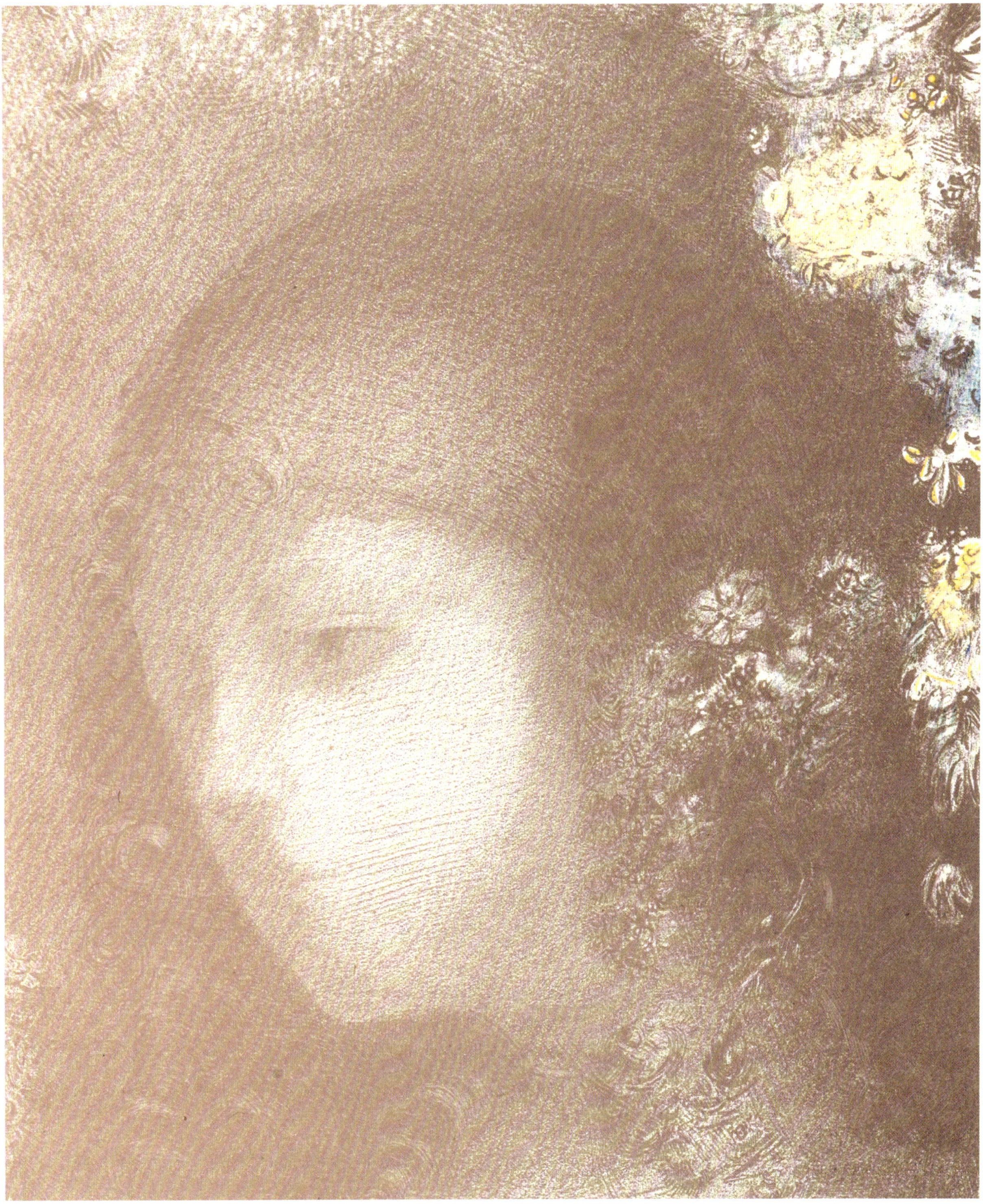

FIG. 23 Odilon Redon, *Child's Head with Flowers*, 1897. Lithograph in brown with color pencil on chine appliqué, 33.8 × 27.4 cm (13 5/16 × 10 13/16 in.). Amsterdam, Van Gogh Museum, p0877N1996

mid-nineteenth century, by the 1890s avant-garde artists had embraced the medium for original artistic expression, influenced in part by publishers such as Vollard. The Impressionists, Neo-Impressionists, Nabis, and Symbolists explored color in their painting practice, believing that color could serve something beyond mimesis to convey scientific principles, emotional states, or symbolic elements. As a relatively easy way to delve into color printing, lithography appealed to them as another avenue through which to extend their chromatic experimentation.

Though Redon had long remained focused on monochrome lithography, like his contemporaries he also ventured into color printing, perhaps encouraged by Vollard, who commissioned *Beatrice* for his 1897 portfolio *The Album of Original Prints from the Vollard Gallery* (*L'album d'estampes originales de la Galerie Vollard*). Redon produced the lithograph with Clot, with whom he had worked for many years and who had established his own atelier around 1895.[12] For this project, Redon remained largely uninvolved in much of the printing process, leaving it in Clot's capable hands. In color lithography, the printer controlled the technical production of color, including the mixing of ink, the separation of the image on different stones, and the registration of color on the paper during printing.

To prepare *Beatrice*, Clot in fact translated an earlier pastel by Redon (fig. 24) into print, simplifying the artist's contour lines and diluting the pastel's vibrant color.[13] He used translucent washes to emphasize Beatrice's ethereal, almost ghostly figure, her long neck and bare shoulders floating against a muted sky. There is a precise application of opaque color in the upper right corner, where vibrant blue organic shapes emerge as if from outside the frame: Perhaps a decorative addition, the markings—more detailed than other color elements in the print—seem to be leaves from a nearby tree. The figure materializes out of swaths of diaphanous color, the contour of her pale-yellow face articulated only by the gray sky against which she is set.

To produce the lithograph, Clot would likely have hand copied the large areas of the composition, in reverse, onto the surface of a stone. He then would have transferred the keystone image onto five or six other stones, which he would have filled in by hand depending on which color the stone would eventually print. From there he would have printed each stone and adjusted the color by comparing it to the original copy, which was in his possession throughout this process.[14] Clot dexterously re-created the texture of the original by translating the powdery and hazy effect of pastel using a lithographic crayon on stone.

A trial proof of *Beatrice* held at the Rijksmuseum offers insight into how both artist and printer translated the color palette of the original

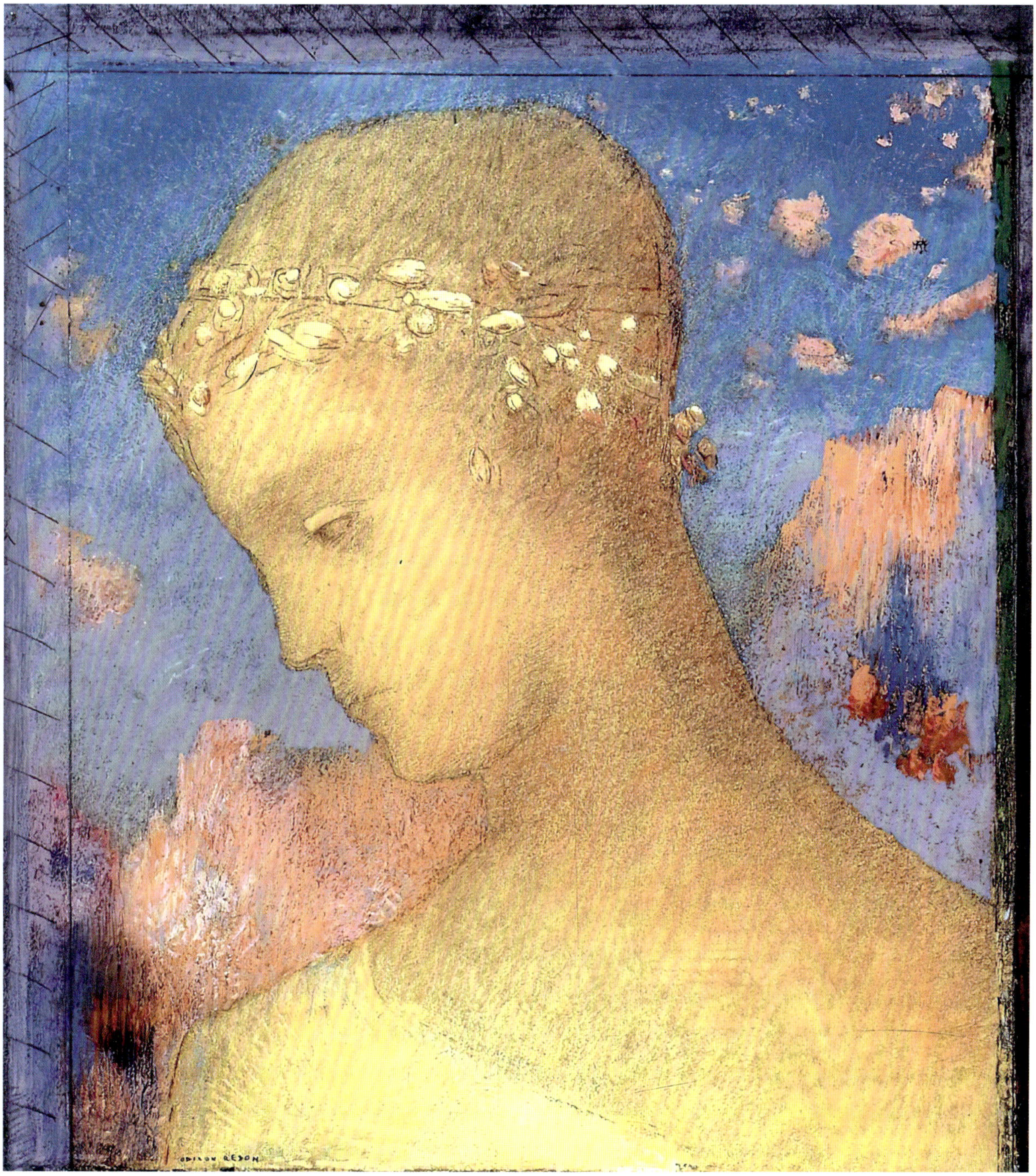

FIG. 24 Odilon Redon, *Beatrice*, 1885. Pastel over traces of charcoal on paper laid down on board, 34.5 × 30 cm (13 ⁹⁄₁₆ × 11 ¹³⁄₁₆ in.). Private collection

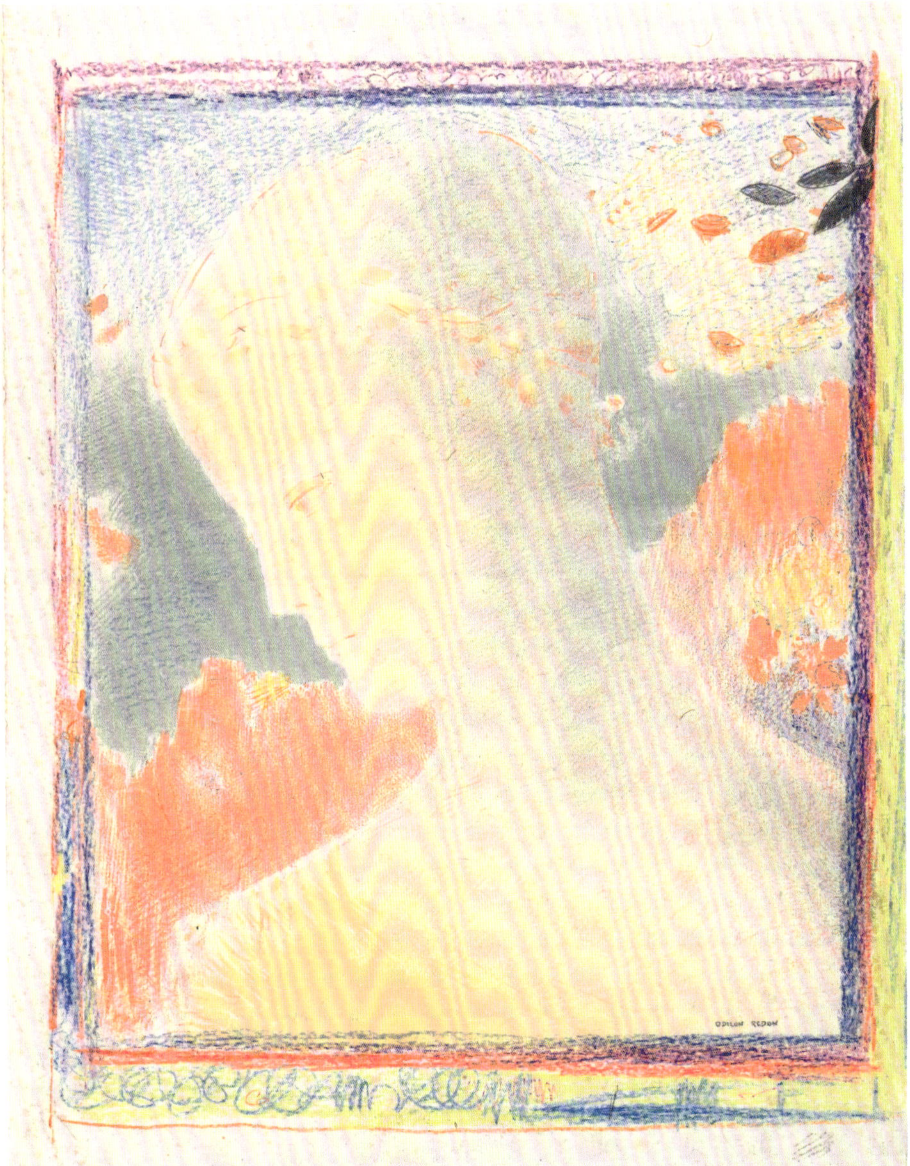

FIG. 25 Odilon Redon, *Beatrice*, 1897. Color lithograph, hand colored with pastels, 38.5 × 32 cm (15 $\frac{3}{16}$ × 12 $\frac{5}{8}$ in.). Amsterdam, Rijksmuseum, RP-P-1971-28

pastel into the lithograph's soft, muted tones, and how Clot translated the composition while simultaneously lightening the color scheme (fig. 25). A subsequent proof now at the Bibliothèque nationale de France reveals the continued simplification of the composition (fig. 26). Gone is the border surrounding the figure, and although the color clearly appears to have been applied with crayon, it has been smoothed, as if rubbed or brushed on the stone. The print's final iteration lightens the scene, and more of the detail behind and around the figure has faded away. Given the subtlety of the lithograph's washed tones, it is possible that Redon, as evidenced by a letter to Clot, participated in the proofing of the final

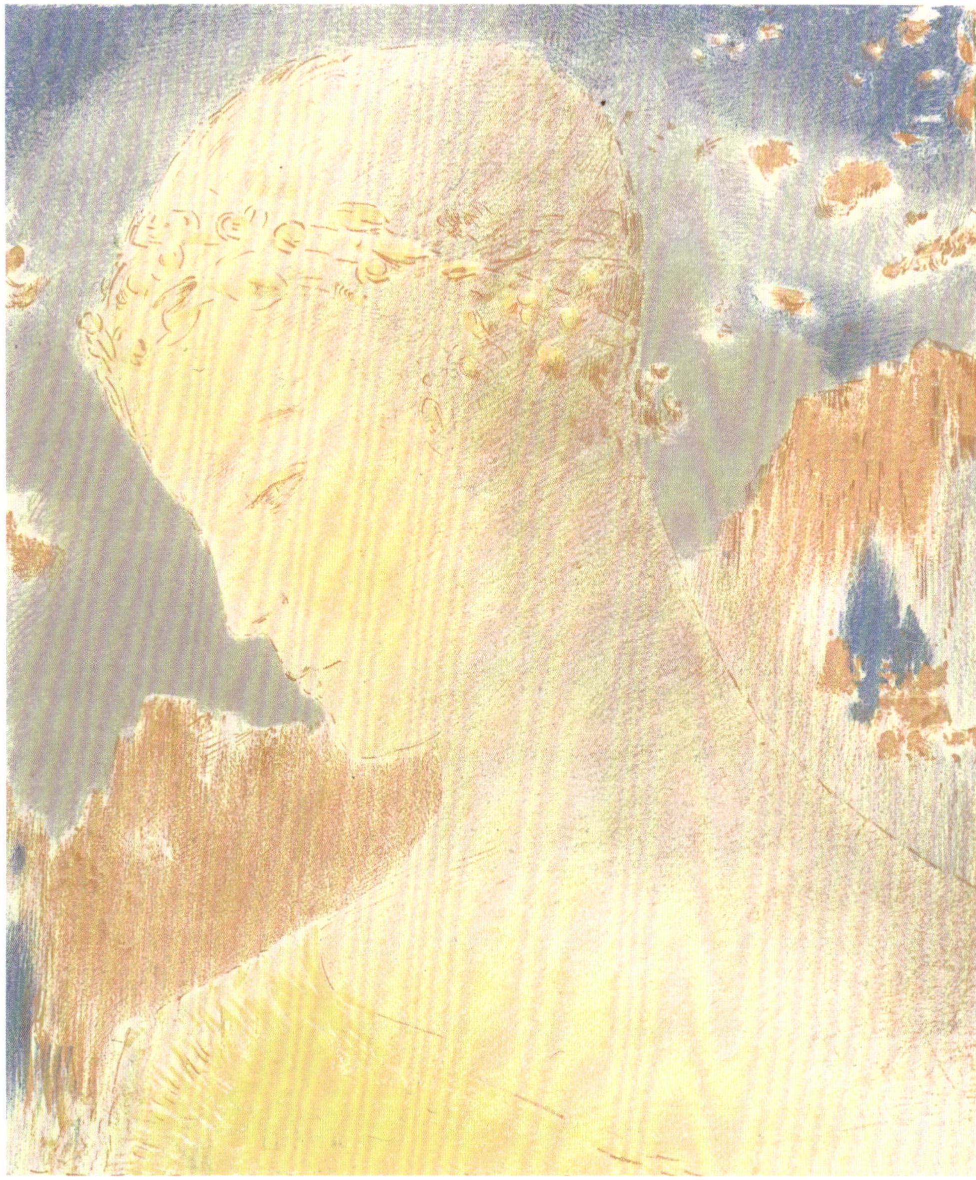

FIG. 26 Odilon Redon, *Beatrice*, 1897. Color lithograph on chine appliqué, Image: 33.5 × 29.5 cm (13 3/16 × 11 5/8 in.). Paris, Bibliothèque nationale de France, Département des estampes et de la photographie

print, visiting the printer's atelier to discuss and work on color and its translation.[15] Clot, however, was the skilled artist behind the transformation of the bolder lines of the trial proof into the subtle blend of the final version's composition.

Despite Clot's hand in producing *Beatrice*, Vollard included the print under Redon's name alone in his album. Its reproductive status, once identified, however, had a significant impact on the way one leading art critic, André Mellerio, interpreted the print. In his 1898 review of Vollard's album, Mellerio describes Redon's lithograph as "a pensive and lofty Beatrice, an exercise in the way of color, a personal and intense lithograph."[16] Mellerio suggests that the artwork's intimacy emerged from Redon's creative process, yet both the design and the color developed from Clot's translation of Redon's original pastel; the print's aesthetics are the result of Clot's simplification of composition, lightening of palette, and delicate washes of color. Realizing later that it was a copy, Mellerio addressed the reproductive quality in his entry on Redon in his 1898 publication *La lithographie originale en couleurs* (Original color lithography), in which he compares *Beatrice* to Redon's only other color lithograph, *The Shulamite* (plate 40):

> Until now Odilon Redon has produced only two color prints. One, his *Beatrice*, in softened, almost misty, colors, with its delicate charm remains almost hesitant. But the other, *La Sulamite*, freshly conceived and boldly harmonious in color, is a find—a new and personal quality is here given to color lithography. This is not a copy, but the equivalent of a pastel, in which the formerly severe wielder of the black crayon now seeks limpid tones and beautiful nuances.[17]

Like *Beatrice*, *The Shulamite* was also printed by Clot in 1897. It depicts the serene figure of a woman featured in the biblical poem Song of Solomon. While Beatrice takes form from color, the Shulamite woman's face is composed of several thin blue lines that demarcate her gentle features as she lowers her head, eyes closed. Employing the reserve, Redon used the craggy texture of the lithographic crayon to further outline her shape with yellow lines, creating a blue and yellow contrast. He printed additional impressions with black ink rather than blue, interweaving black and yellow at the base of the print (fig. 27). Applying delicate lines throughout, Redon used lithography to extend his drawing practice, creating a composition through line, rather than washes of color.

The differences in how Clot and Redon executed and applied color may account for Mellerio's distinction between *Beatrice* and *The Shulamite*. Whereas Clot applied color in swaths, Redon executed his in the form of hand-drawn lines. Although experienced in printing monochrome lithographs, Redon may have been reluctant to explore the more technical aspects of color lithography, including the creation of color through washes on the stone or the layering of color to produce new tones—techniques Clot employed in the "copy" of *Beatrice*. Rather, Redon crafted color through line to make an "equivalent" to his pastels. Nevertheless, the artist had long understood the potential for lithography to translate his drawings into print and thus circulate his aesthetic more widely. So perhaps the reproductive quality that Mellerio disparaged in his

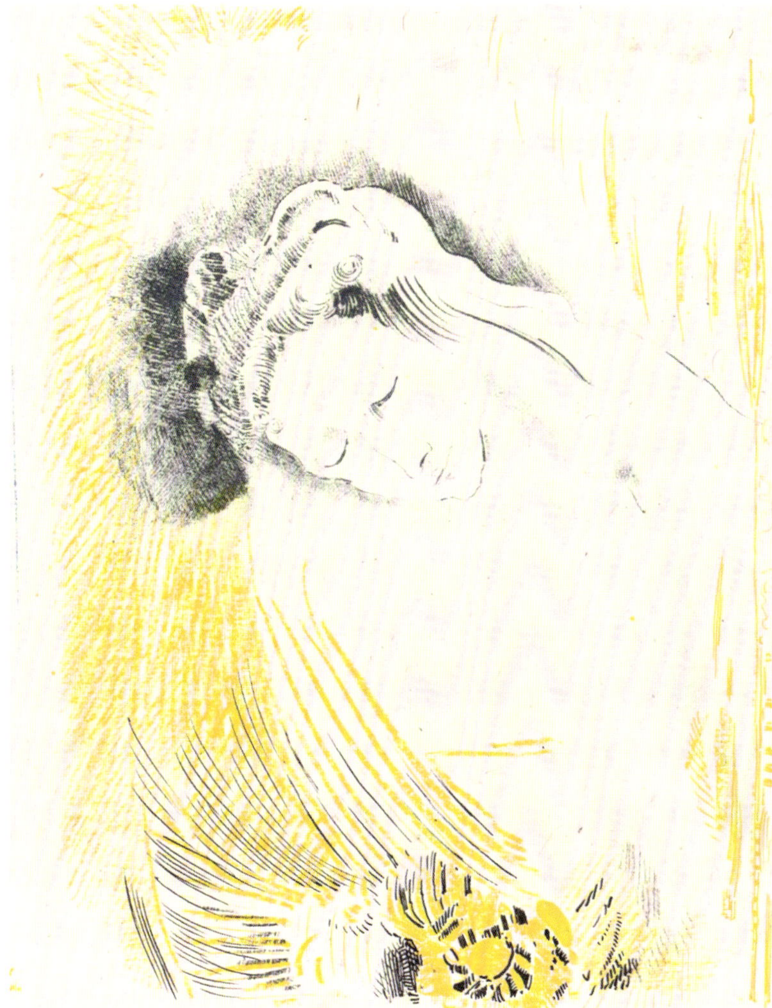

FIG. 27 Odilon Redon, *The Shulamite*, 1897. Lithograph printed in black and yellow on heavy cream chine, Image: 25.2 × 20.2 cm (9 15/16 × 8 in.). Art Institute of Chicago, The Stickney Collection, 1920.1815

review of *Beatrice* would have been seen by the artist as a benefit, along with Clot's ability to capture the "beautiful nuances" of pastel in print.

By the end of the 1890s, Redon had stopped working in color lithography. Perhaps he felt that he had to give up too much control of color in the process and that he had to rely too heavily on Clot's technical expertise and hand. Alternatively, he may have felt he had finally exhausted his lithographic practice, finding himself ready to turn away from black ink on paper and apply his creative attentions more fully to color—its vibrant energy and powerful clashes—through oil on canvas and pastel on paper.

Notes

Translations mine unless otherwise noted.

1 Redon 1961 [1869], 160.

2 For more on this history, see Mainardi 2017, 14–21. The official Salon was the state-sponsored institution behind the production, display, and circulation of art that dominated the art world in France from the seventeenth through the nineteenth century. For more, see Jensen 1994; and Mainardi 1993. See also Bann 2001.

3 Steam-powered machines became widespread in the second half of the nineteenth century, and most chromolithographs circulating in the public sphere—including mass-produced trade cards, posters, calendars, and labels—were printed using steam-powered machine presses and with inexpensive materials. See Kalba 2017.

4 Giviskos 2018, 76.

5 See Rosen 1988.

6 Redon had a complex working relationship with printers. He was at times frustrated by their involvement while also reliant on their skill and expertise. See Gott 1990C, 42–44.

7 Pat Gilmour believes that Clot printed *Christ* when he was working at Lemercier or already thinking of establishing his own practice, which he did around 1895 (see note 12). Copies of this work were in the printer's atelier when he died in 1936. See Gilmour 1988, 134.

8 Gott 1990A, 29. Original quote is from Redon 1986 [1922], 124.

9 Gott 1990A, 30.

10 Gott 1990A, 30.

11 See Figura 2005.

12 Around 1895 Clot left Lemercier and opened his own atelier, where he specialized in artistic lithographs, excelling at color lithography. Once he was established, painter-printmakers sought him out, as did print publishers who were willing to pay the high cost for his expertise. See Lauricella 2022.

13 Vollard commissioned a reproduction of a work from his own collection, having purchased the pastel from Redon in 1896 for 150 francs. He noted the purchase on October 29 in his ledger book: "Bought from Redon a pastel called Beatrice" (Acheté à Redon un pastel Béatrice). Vollard Archives, MS 241 (4,3), fol. 56, Documentation Center, Musée d'Orsay, Paris.

14 A letter sent to Clot by Camille Redon, the artist's wife, refers to the pastel and asks about its whereabouts. Camille Redon to Auguste Clot, December 14, 1896, Auguste Clot Collection, Department of Prints and Photography, Bibliothèque nationale de France, Paris.

15 In a letter to Clot dated April 13, 1897, Redon writes, "Dear Monsieur Clot, I think it will be good if I am present for the printing of trial proofs of the pastel M. Vollard is reproducing. There will undoubtedly be some color to change or modify. I am therefore at your disposal for the day and time, except Friday." (Cher monsieur Clot, je crois qu'il sera bien que je sois présent aux essais du pastel reproduit de M. Vollard. Il y aura sans doute quelque couleur à changer ou à modifier. Je suis donc à votre disposition pour le jour et l'heure, sauf le vendredi.) Odilon Redon to Auguste Clot, April 13, 1897, Auguste Clot Collection, Department of Prints and Photography, Bibliothèque nationale de France, Paris.

16 "Odilon Redon, une *Béatrice* d'allure pensive et haute, essai dans la voie de la couleur, du si personnel et intense lithographe." Mellerio 1898, 10. The review is of Vollard's second album of prints by *peintres-graveurs*.

17 Mellerio 1978 [1898], 88.

PLATES

Noir

In the mid-nineteenth century, a rise in the availability of dark drawing materials led many French artists to more boldly explore the power and narrative richness of black. Inspired by Rembrandt's haunting chiaroscuro and the evocative darkness in the art of Francisco Goya, they saw endless possibilities in black media, whether crafting Realist scenes of urban strife or phantasmagoric visions. Although working in varied styles, these artists shared an experimental approach to their materials, using viscous ink and powdery charcoal to create effects of smoke, dirt, and mysterious atmosphere.

Redon applied the term *noirs* to his own expressive endeavors with black media. The darkness of the materials was suited to his indeterminate visual world, teeming with shadows and strange apparitions. The limited palette drove him to technical innovation; he found new and distinctive ways to depict the complex interplay of light and dark. For his drawings, made primarily in charcoal with additions of black chalk and black pastel, he employed shades of black as a full spectrum of color, attaining a wide variety of tones and textures. He often further manipulated the media—rubbing, wiping, and scratching the surface to achieve a range of atmospheric effects. Out of these tenebrous drawings emerged an array of nightmares, including spectral figures (plate 1), dismantled skeletons (plate 2), and disembodied eyes (plate 3).

With lithography, Redon created equally dramatic effects of contrast between the dense black printing ink and the stark white paper. His approximately 170 monochrome prints, inspired by literary and religious texts as well as his own frightening visions, explore many of the same surreal motifs as the *noir* drawings. In prints like *Christ* (plate 4), Redon used delicate hatching and subtle gradations of tone to imbue his monochromatic images with depth and emotion. Rather than acting as a constraint, the limited spectrum of the *noirs* helped the artist develop a distinct pictorial language and affinity for invention that he would retain throughout his career.

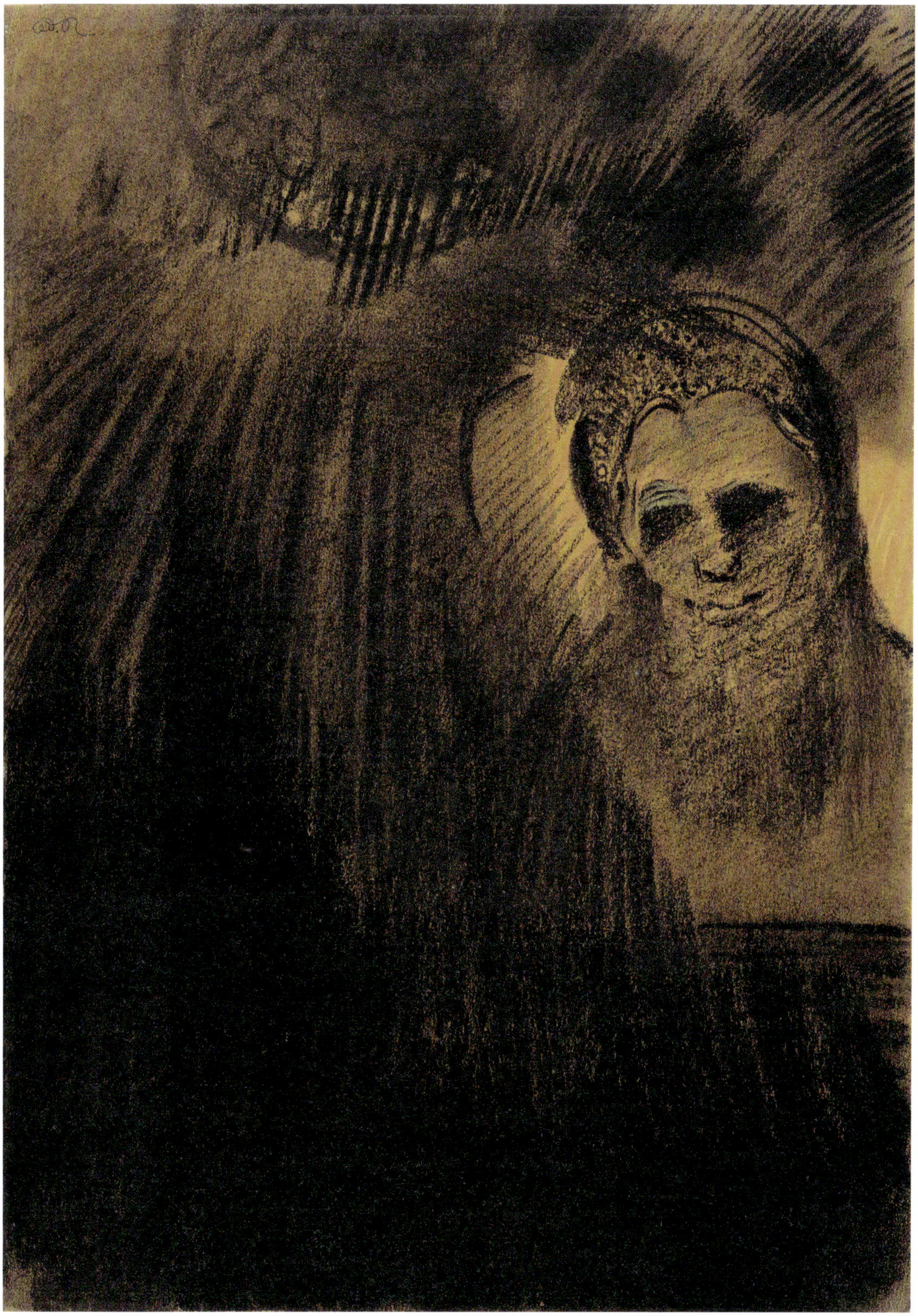

1
Apparition, ca. 1880–90

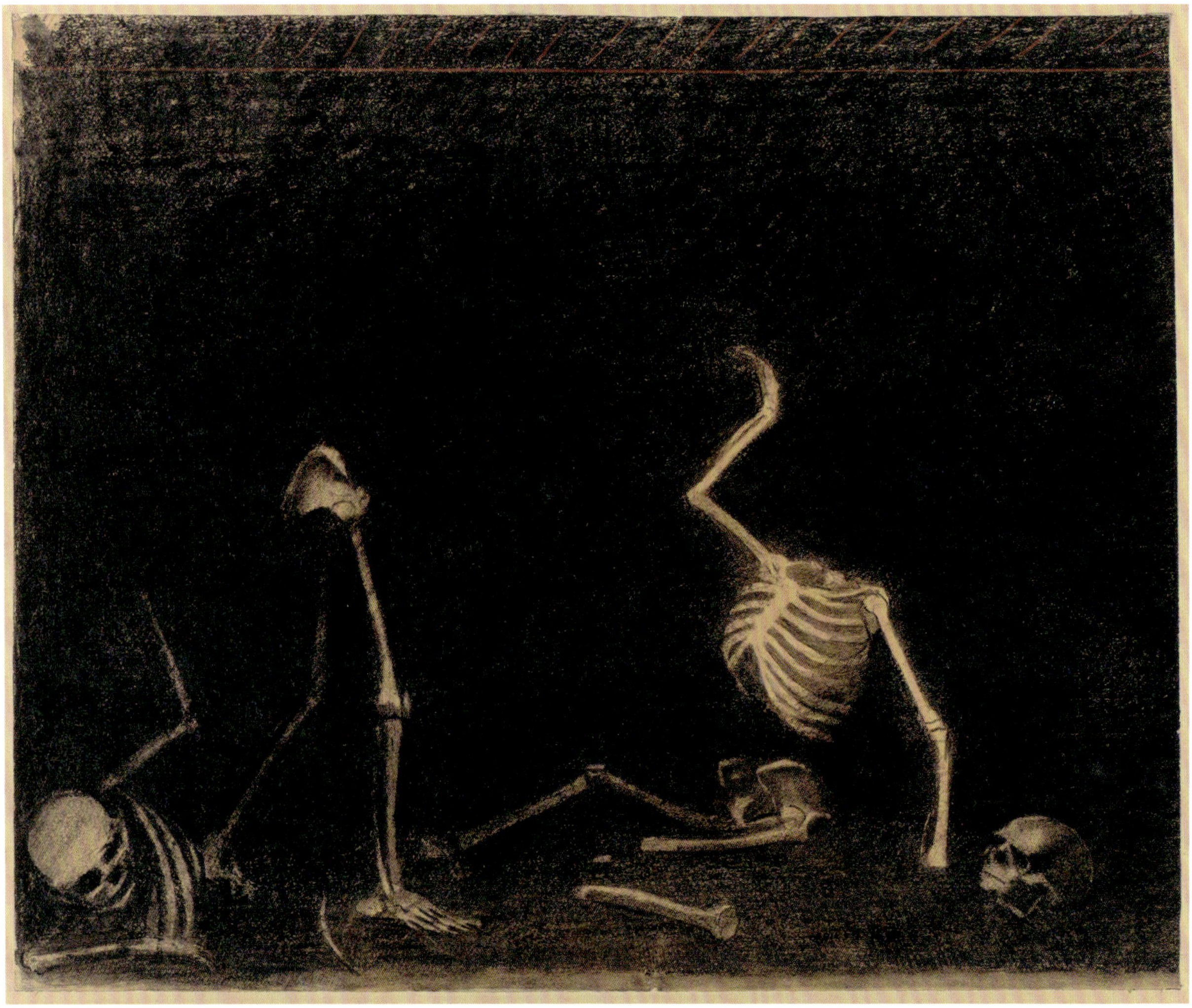

2
The Battle of the Bones, ca. 1881

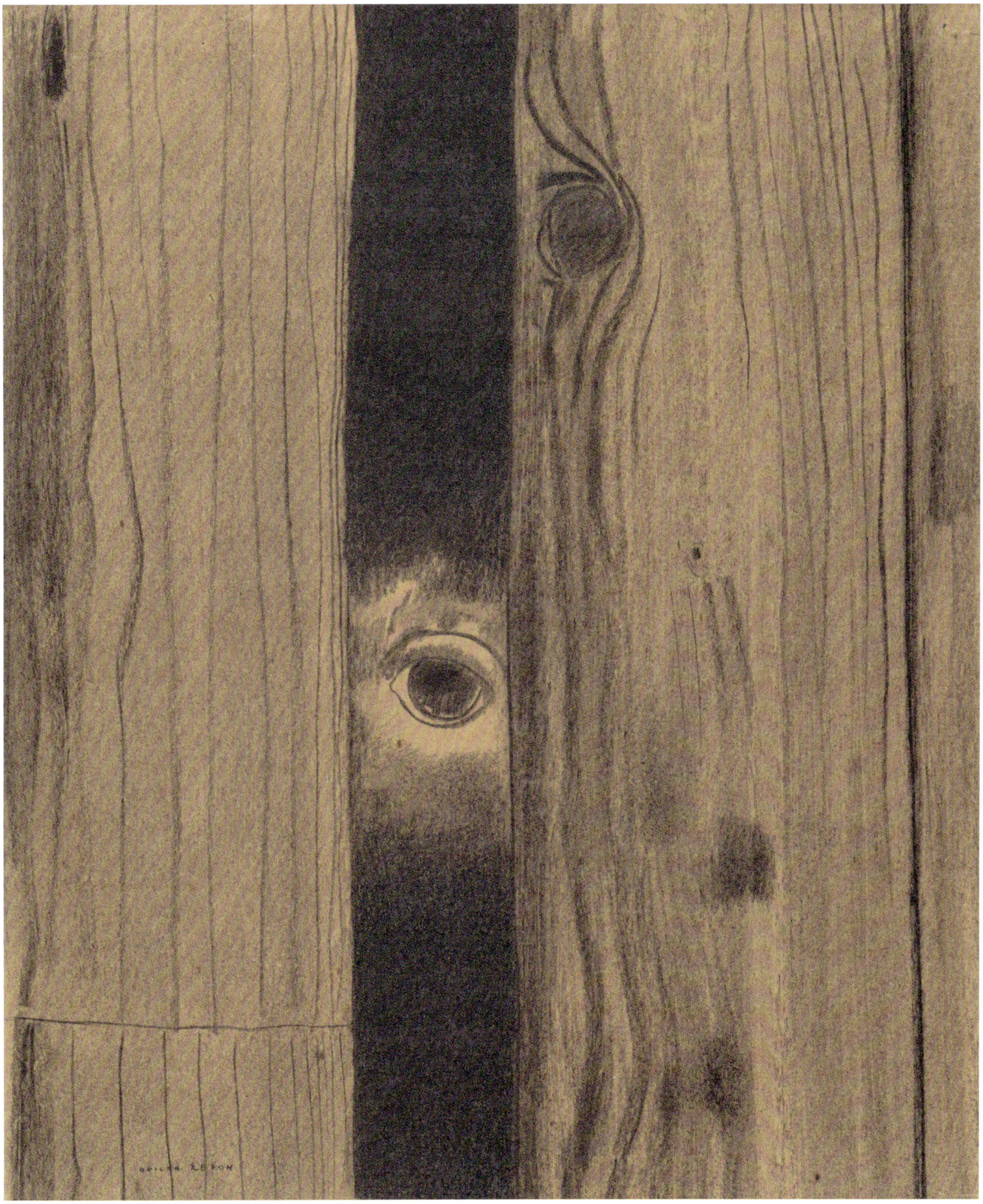

3
The Tell-Tale Heart, 1883

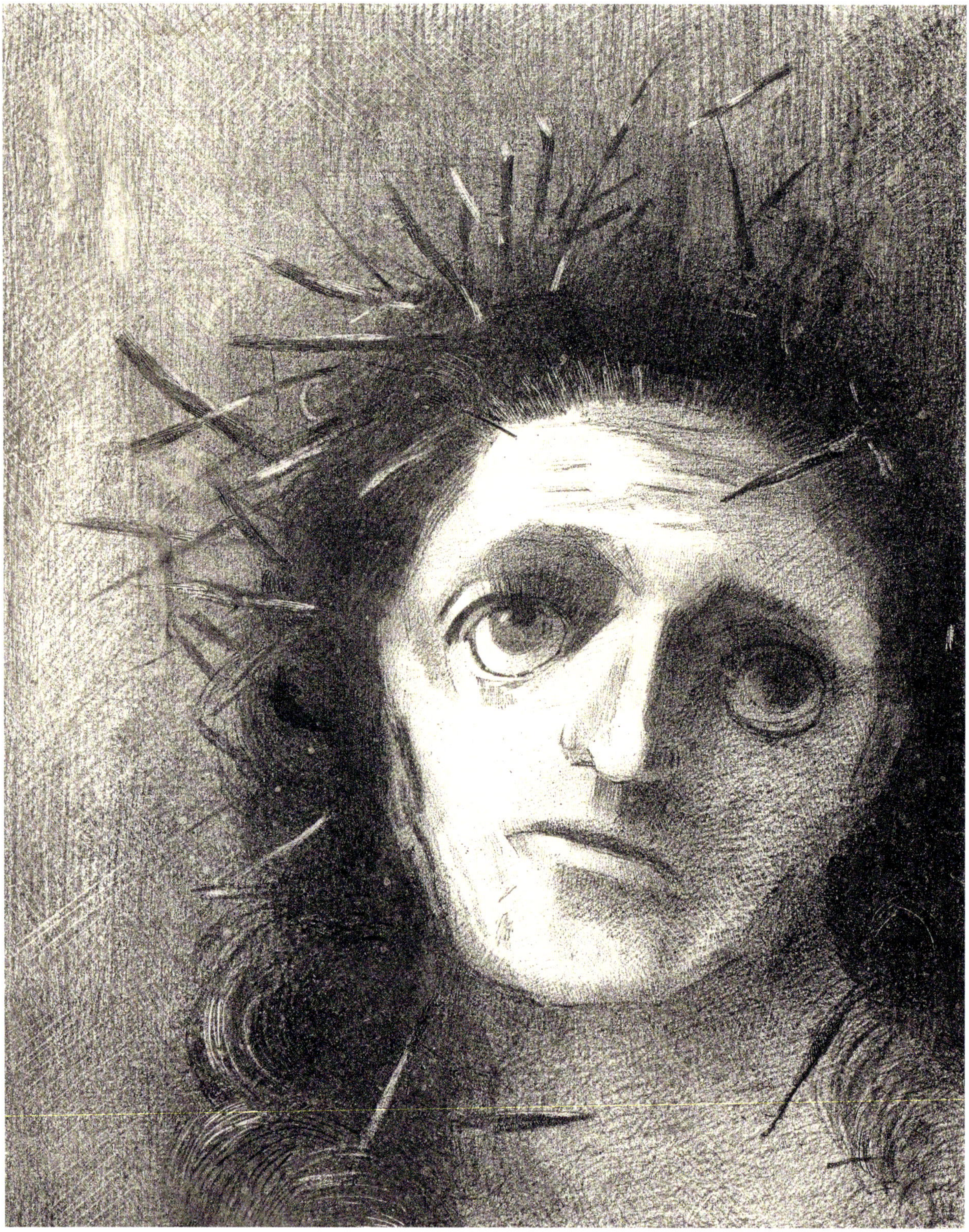

4
Christ, 1887

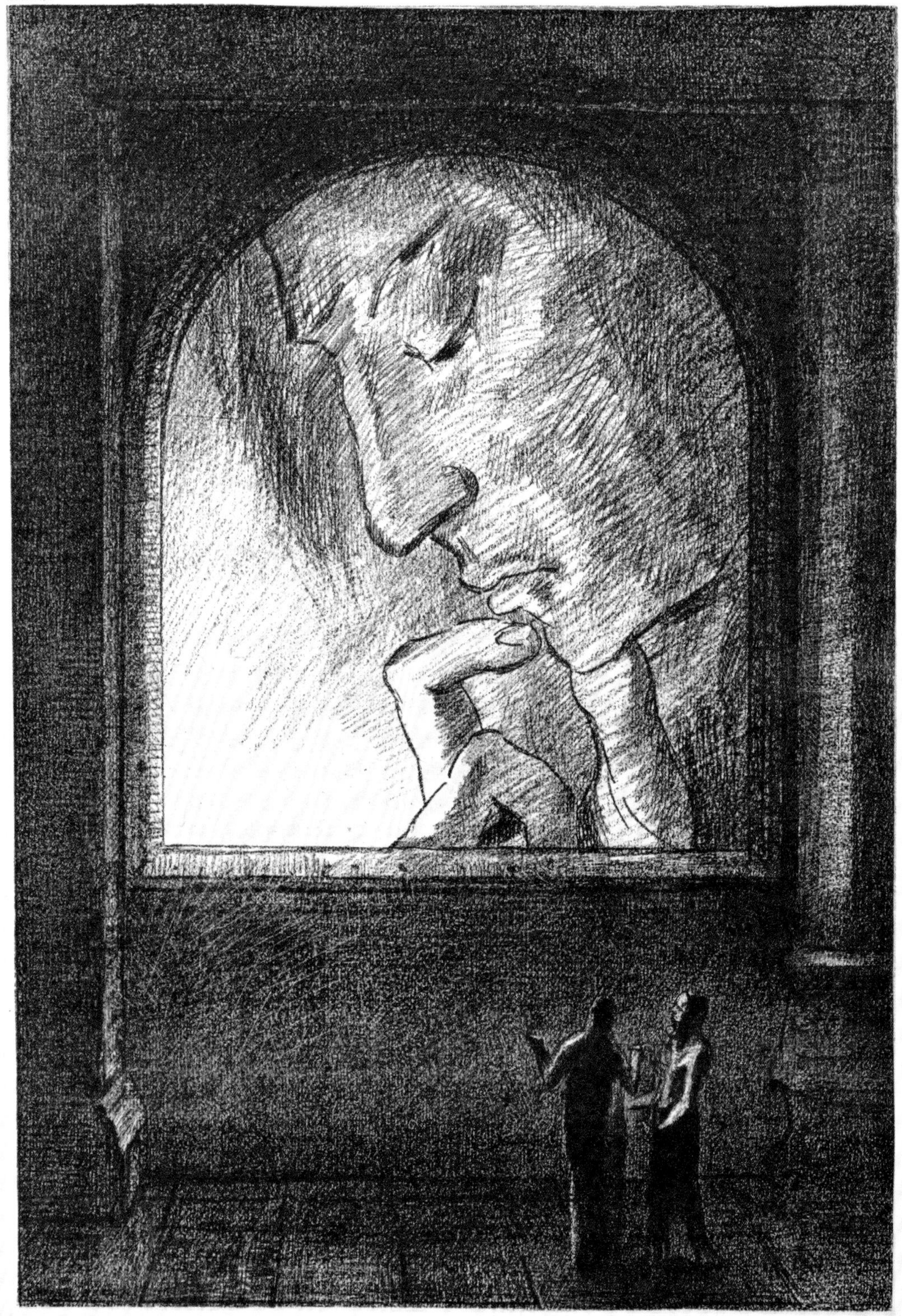

5
Light, 1893

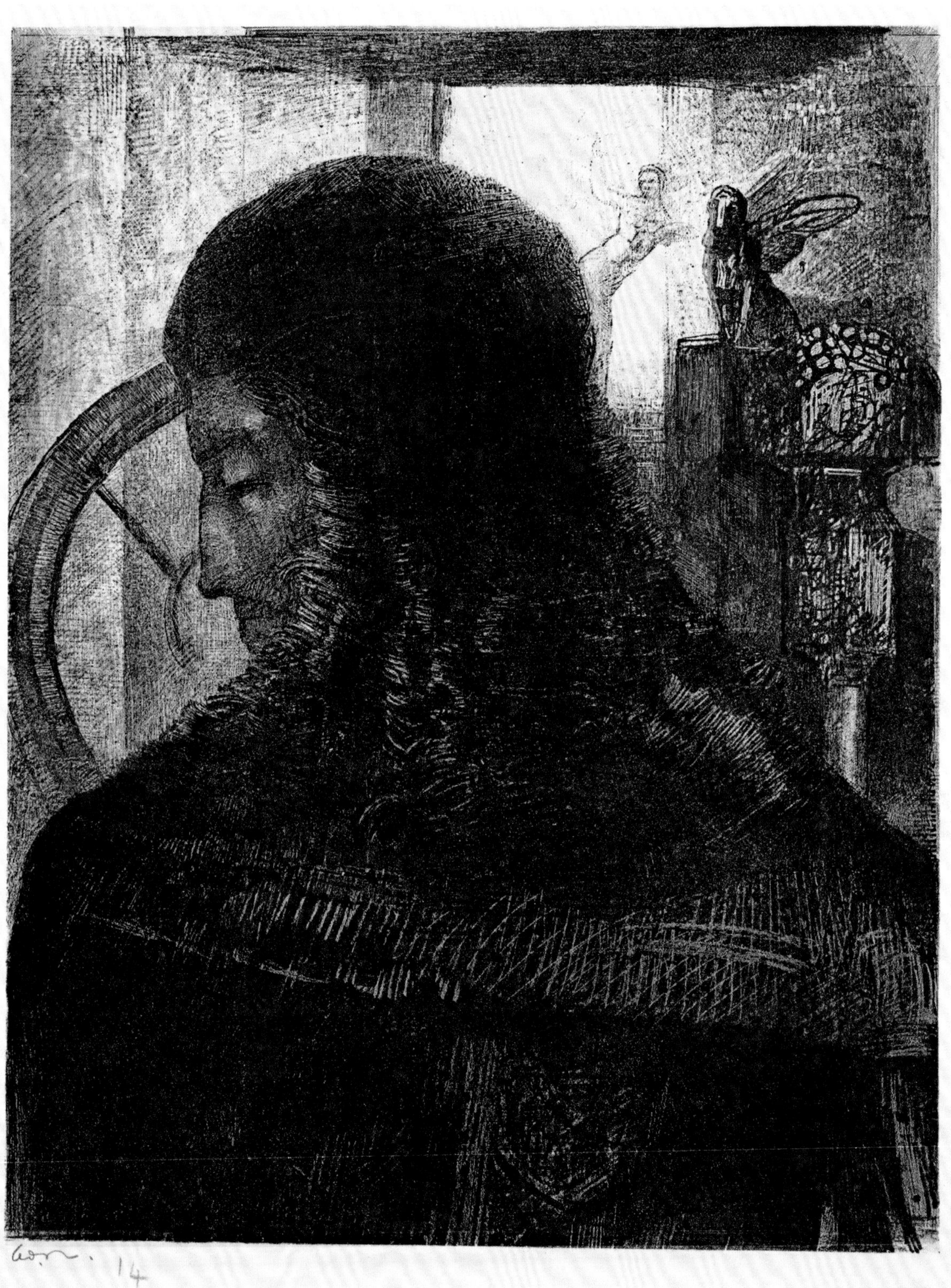

6
Old Knight, 1896

Temptation of Saint Anthony

Throughout his career Redon employed the lithographic portfolio as a medium to engage with authors like Charles Baudelaire and Edgar Allan Poe, whose macabre writing shares similarities with the artist's other-worldly imagery. This suite of ten lithographs is the first of three portfolios that Redon made inspired by Gustave Flaubert's surreal novel *La tentation de Saint Antoine* (*The Temptation of Saint Anthony*, 1874). Published in 1888, 1889, and 1896, the portfolios include thirty-nine prints and three cover pages, representing almost a quarter of the artist's lithographic oeuvre. Redon was first inspired to illustrate the book at the suggestion of his close friend the Symbolist critic Emile Hennequin, who told him he would find "new monsters" in its pages. The project offered Redon another opportunity to interpret a fantastical text and to further establish his reputation among the literary avant-garde in Paris.

Flaubert's *La tentation* is based on the legend of the third-century saint, who lived as a hermit in the Egyptian desert. The novel recounts the events of a single night as Anthony is confronted by a series of terrifying and enticing visions orchestrated by the devil. Saint Anthony's harrowing experience in the desert was a popular subject for artists; by depicting it Redon aligned himself with past visionaries who had represented the story, such as the fifteenth-century engraver Martin Schöngauer and the artist Hieronymus Bosch, who painted a dramatic triptych of the saint's torments in the early sixteenth century. Redon was captivated by Flaubert's richly descriptive contemporary interpretation of the legend, which inspired his surreal compositions.

While Redon had previously produced imagery loosely related to literature, these prints are distinguished by descriptive captions taken directly from Flaubert's novel. Despite this, the works are not illustrations of the text in the traditional sense. Instead, the ambiguous nature of Redon's dark, shadowy prints often means that the captions help to interpret the image. Drawing on the strange and monstrous imagery from his earlier *noirs*, Redon compiled an idiosyncratic grouping of visual motifs, including a hybrid human-fish creature (plate 12) and a baying chimera (plate 14). The pictorial narrative does, however, remain grounded in Christian ideology, ending—like the novel—with an image of Jesus Christ surrounded by the corona of the sun (plate 17), which resembles one of Redon's characteristic floating eyes.

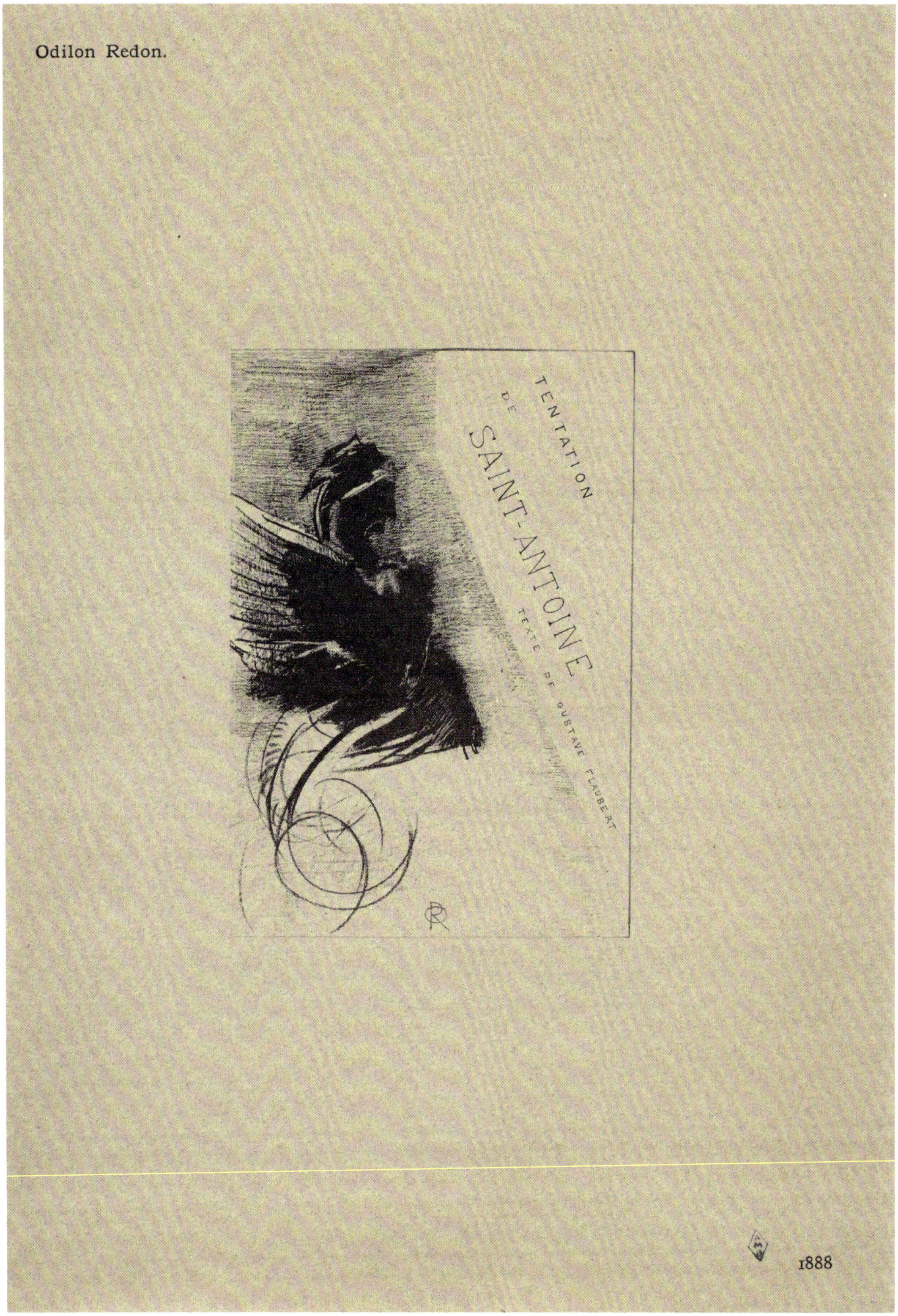

7
Cover of *Temptation of Saint Anthony*, 1888

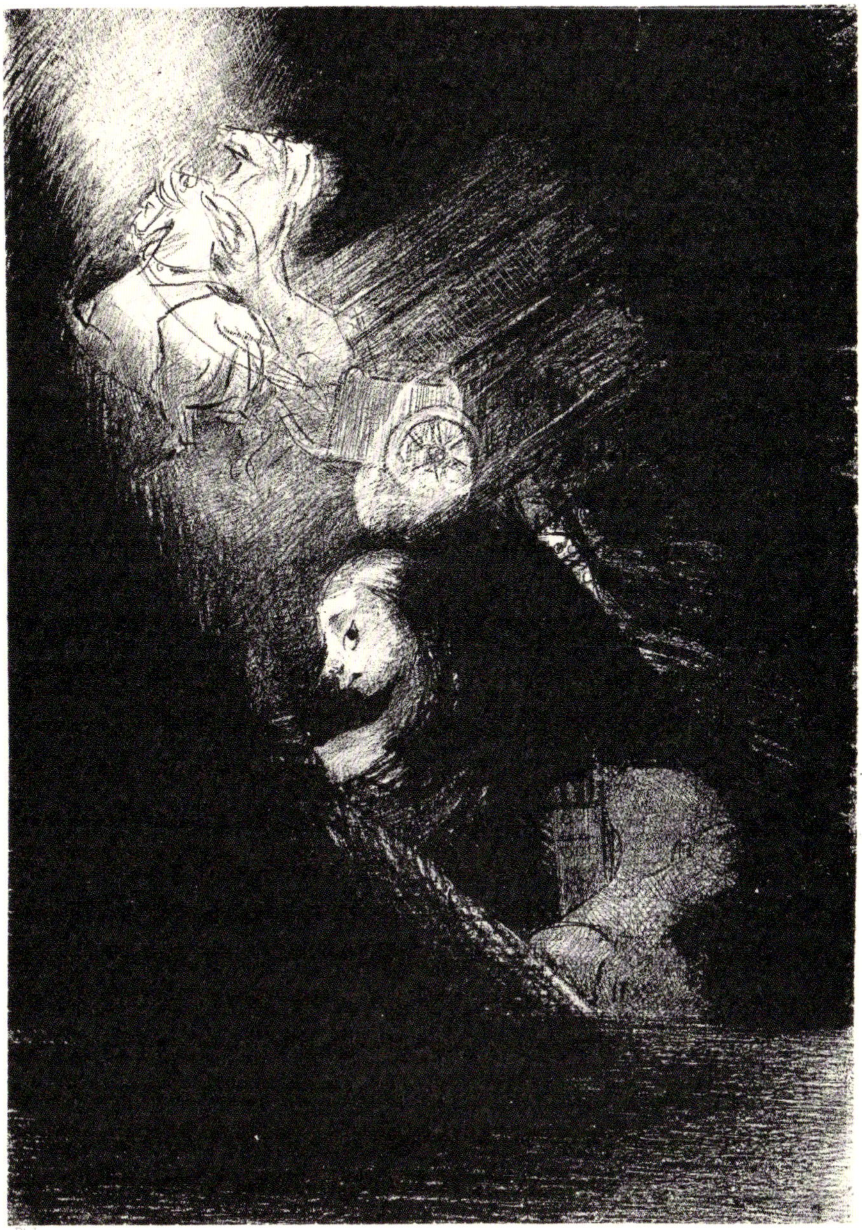

Pl. I.

..... d'abord une flaque d'eau, ensuite une prostituée, le coin d'un temple, une figure de soldat,
un char avec deux chevaux blancs qui se cabrent.

8

First a Pool of Water, Then a Prostitute, the Corner of a Temple, a Soldier's Face, a Chariot with Two White, Rearing Horses, 1888
Plate I from the portfolio *Temptation of Saint Anthony*

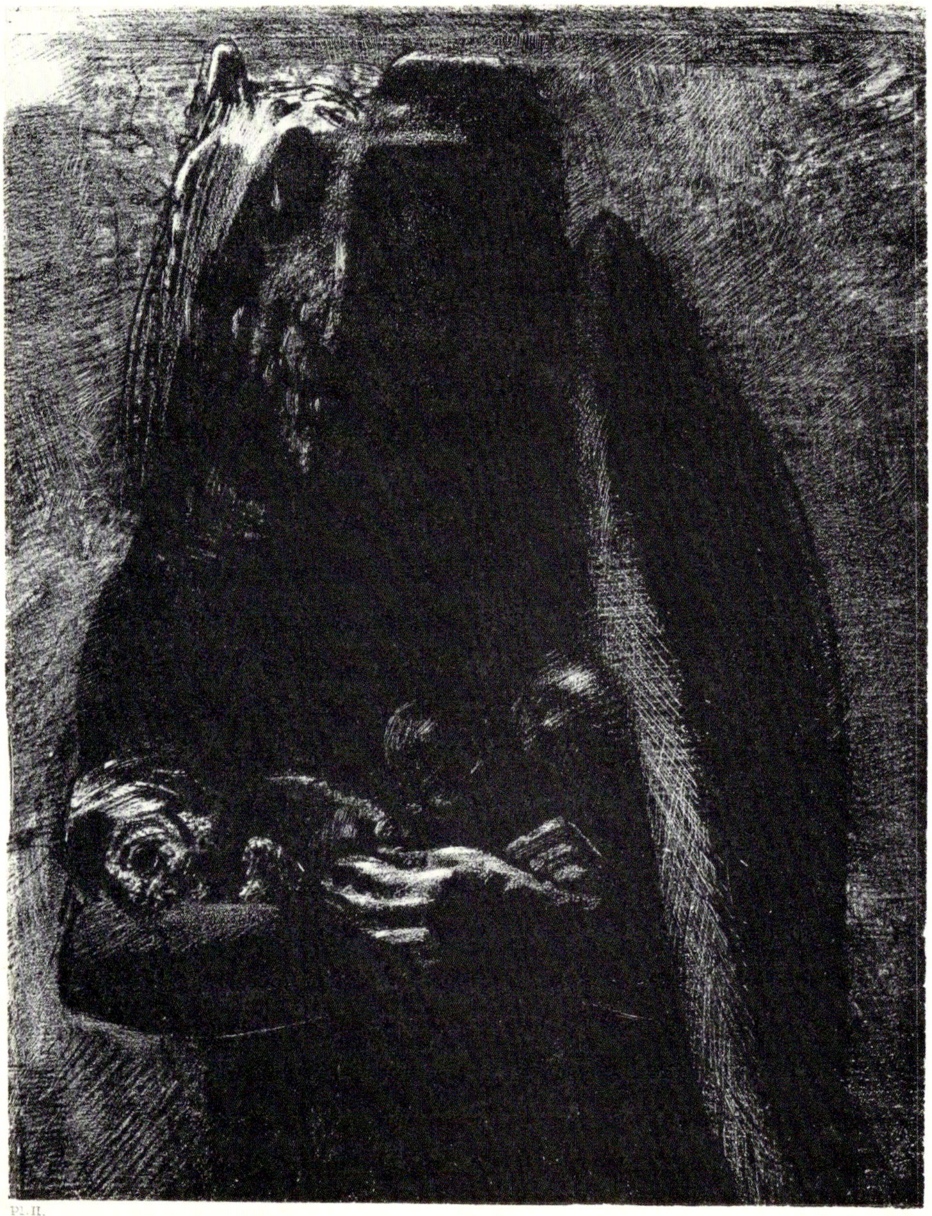

Pl. II.

C'est le diable, portant sous ses deux ailes les sept péchés capitaux.....

9
It Is the Devil, Bearing Beneath His Two Wings the Seven Deadly Sins, 1888
Plate II from the portfolio *Temptation of Saint Anthony*

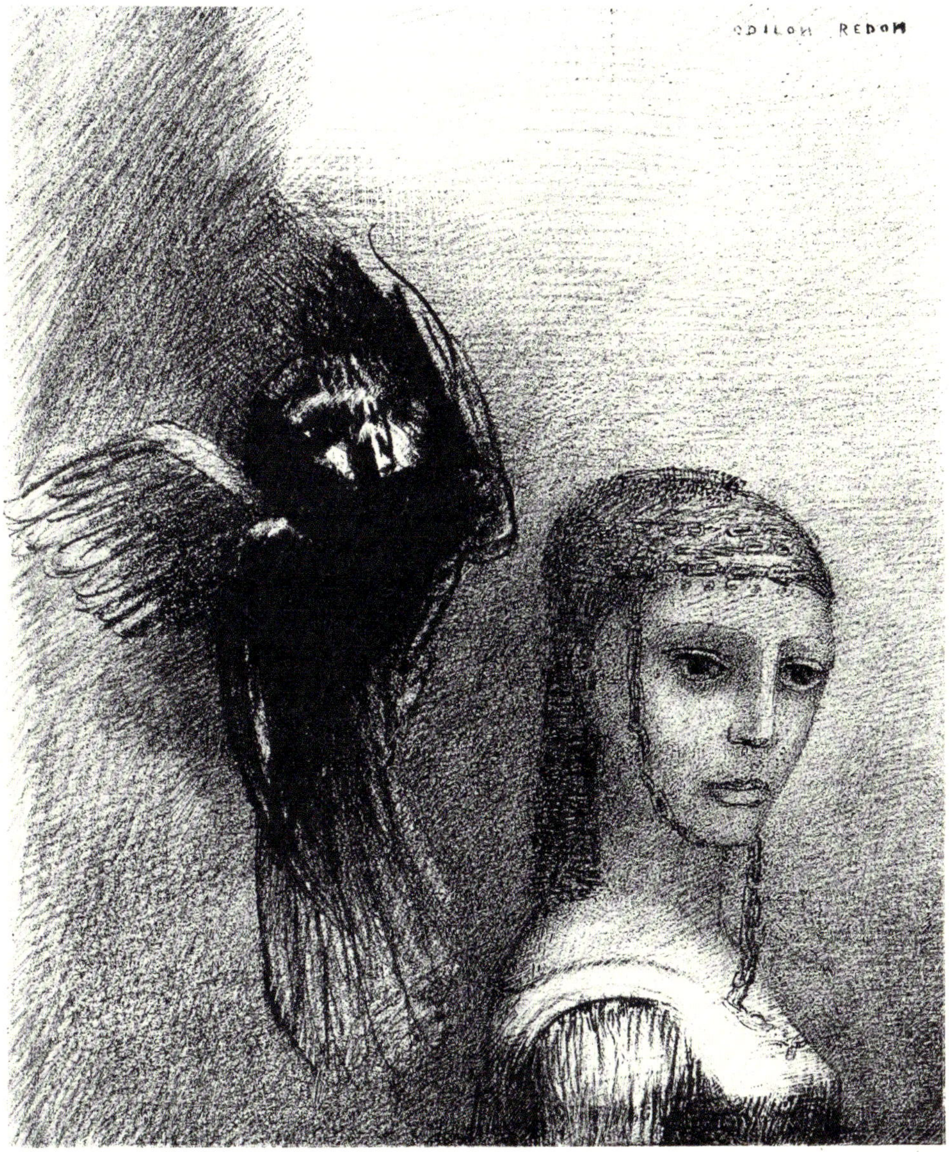

Pl. III.

.... et un grand oiseau, qui descend du ciel, vient s'abattre sur le sommet de sa chevelure.....

10

And a Large Bird, Descending from the Sky, Hurls Itself Against the Topmost Point of Her Hair, 1888
Plate III from the portfolio *Temptation of Saint Anthony*

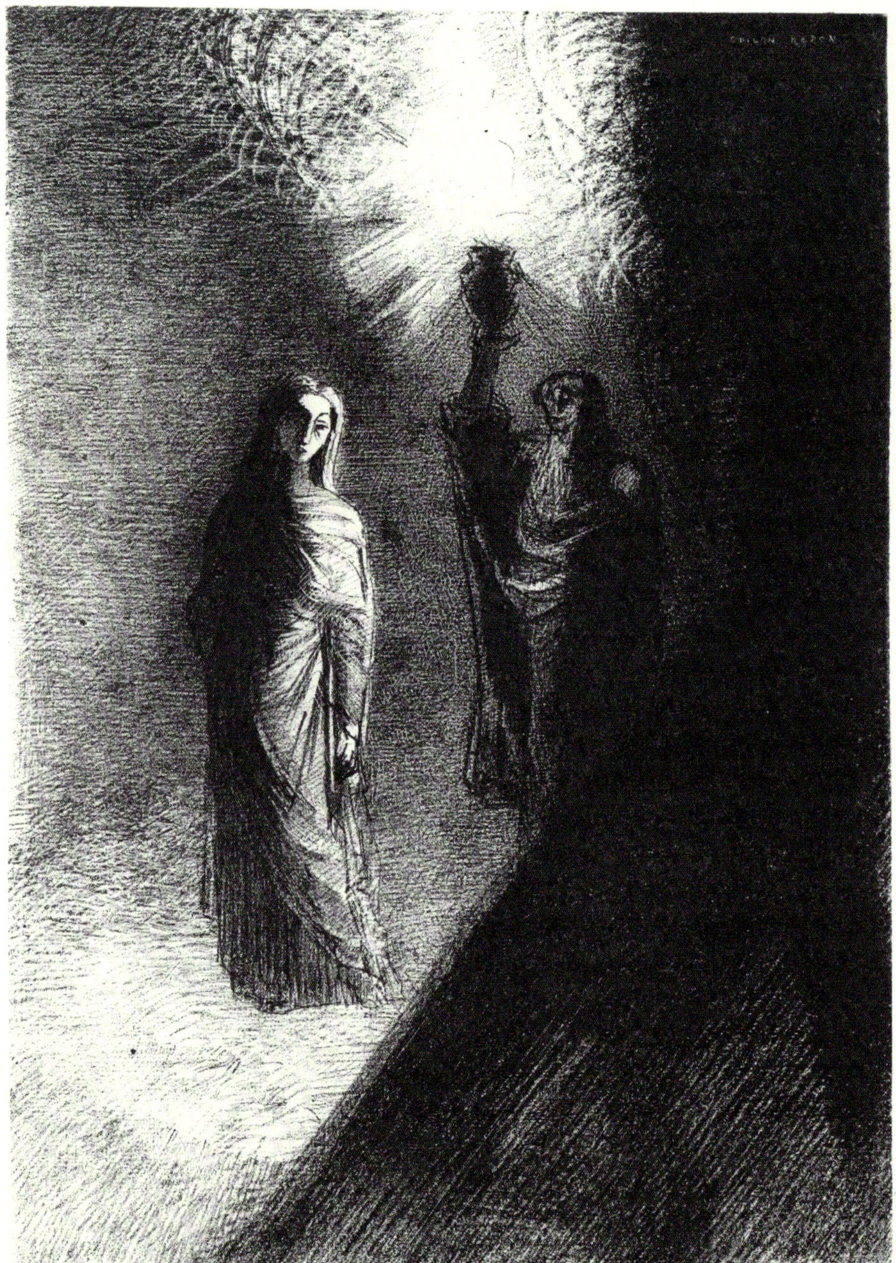

Pl. IV.

Il hausse le vase d'airain.

11
He Raises the Bronze Urn, 1888
Plate IV from the portfolio *Temptation of Saint Anthony*

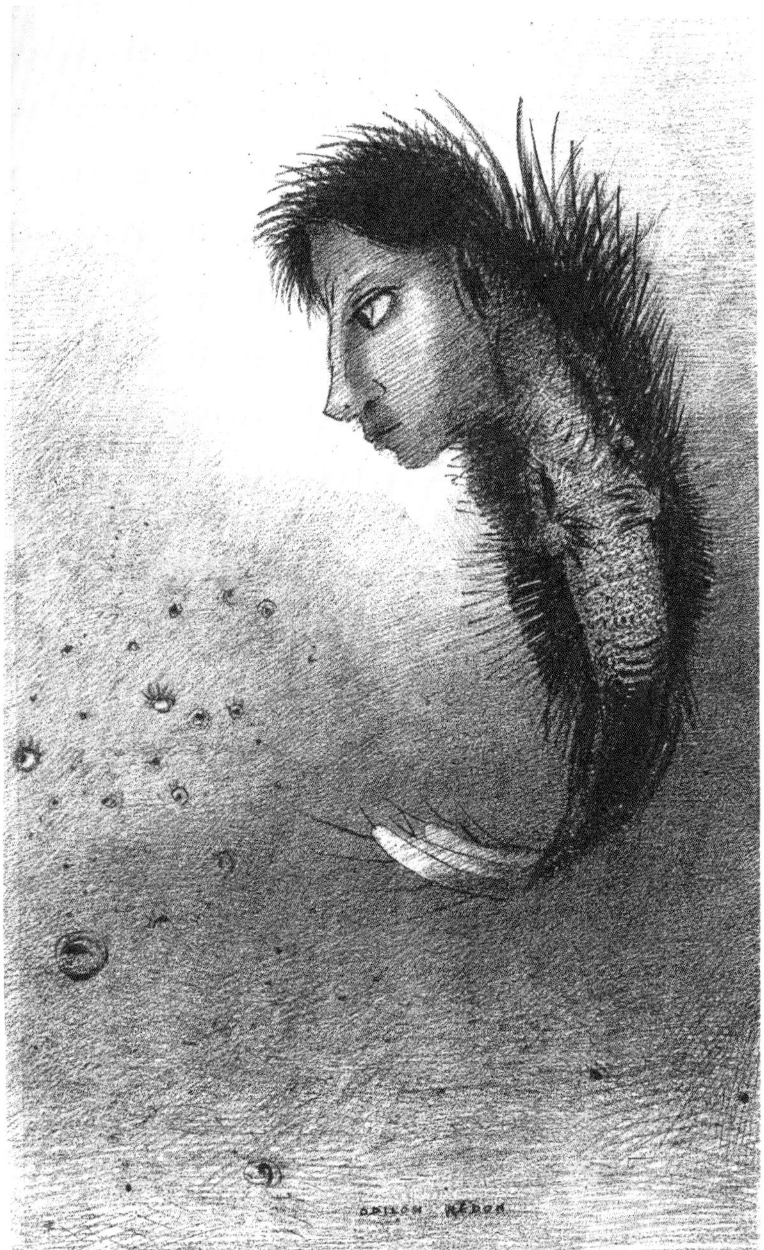

Pl V

Ensuite, paraît un être singulier, ayant une tête d'homme sur un corps de poisson.

12

Then There Appears a Singular Being, Having the Head of a Man on the Body of a Fish, 1888
Plate V from the portfolio *Temptation of Saint Anthony*

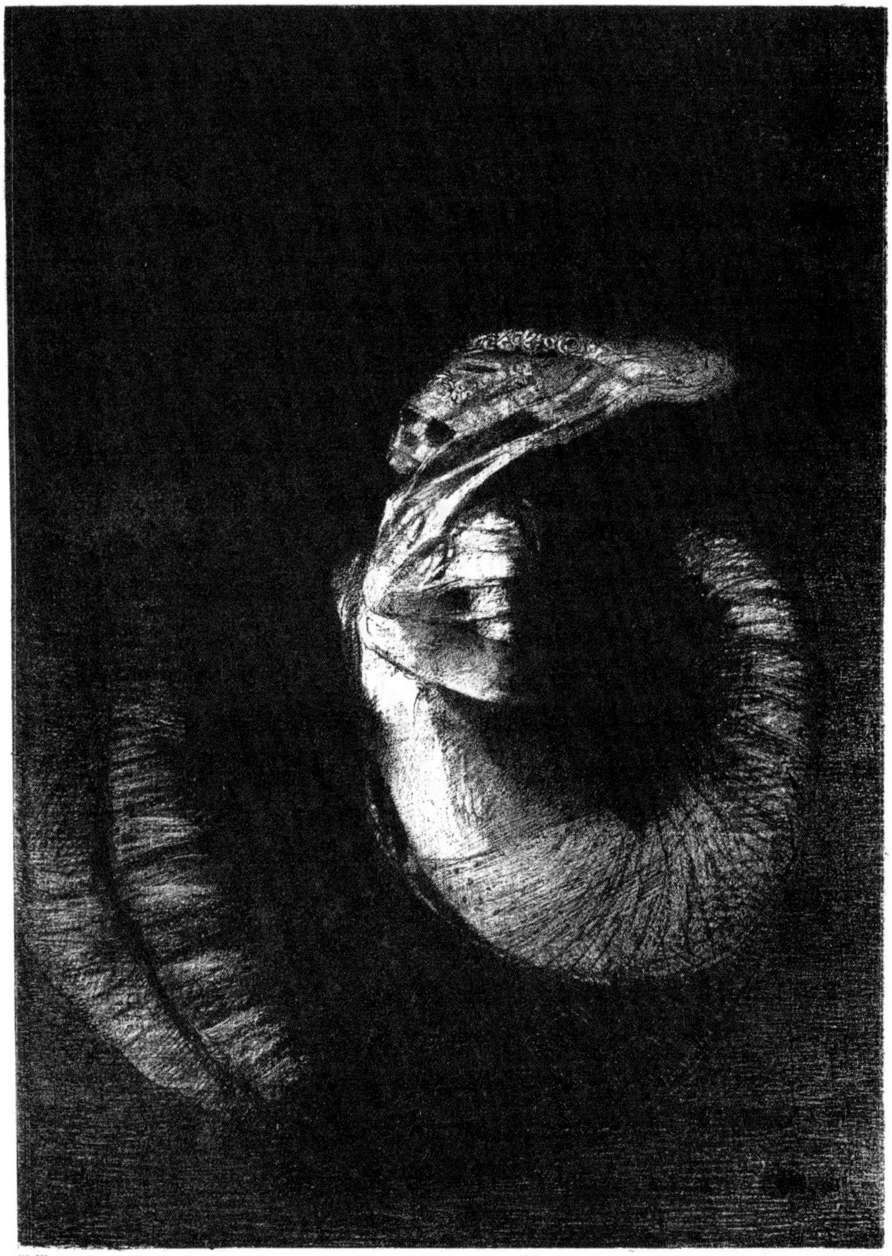

Pl. VI.

C'est une tête de mort, avec une couronne de roses. Elle domine un torse de femme d'une blancheur nacrée.

13
It Is a Skull Wreathed with Roses. It Dominates a Woman's Torso of Pearly Whiteness, 1888
Plate VI from the portfolio *Temptation of Saint Anthony*

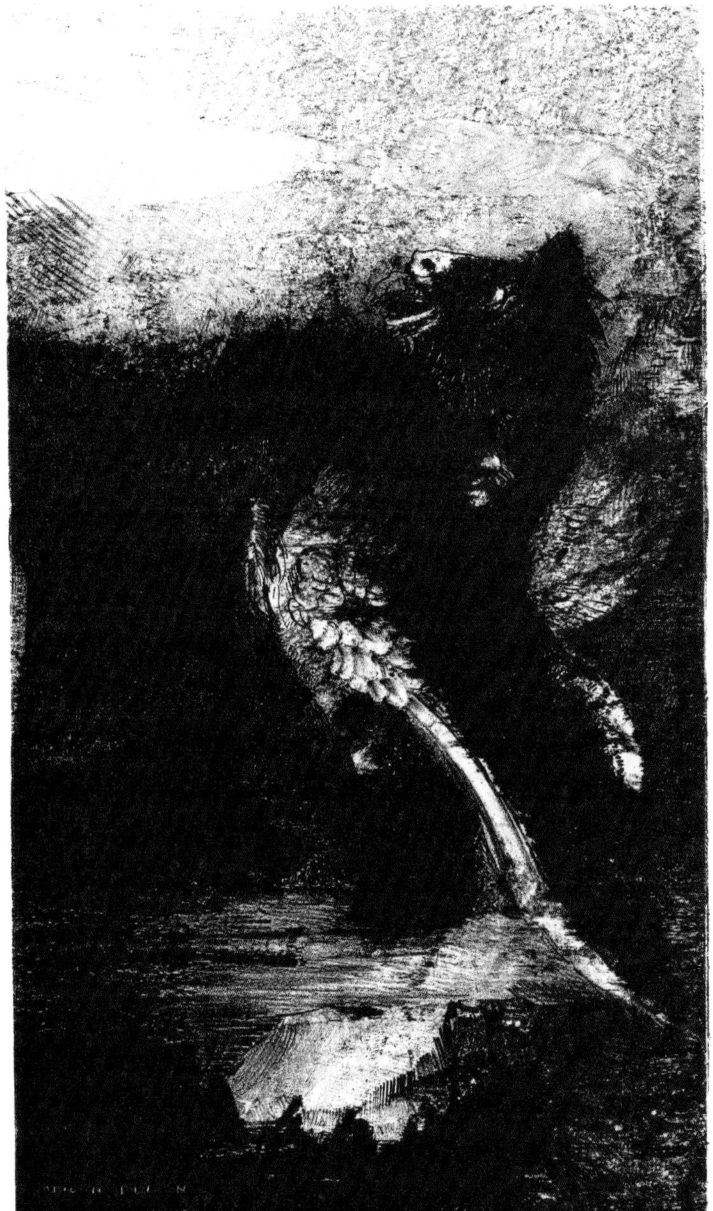

Pl VII.

. . . . . la Chimère aux yeux verts, tournoie, aboie.

14

The Chimera with Green Eyes Turns, Bays, 1888
Plate VII from the portfolio *Temptation of Saint Anthony*

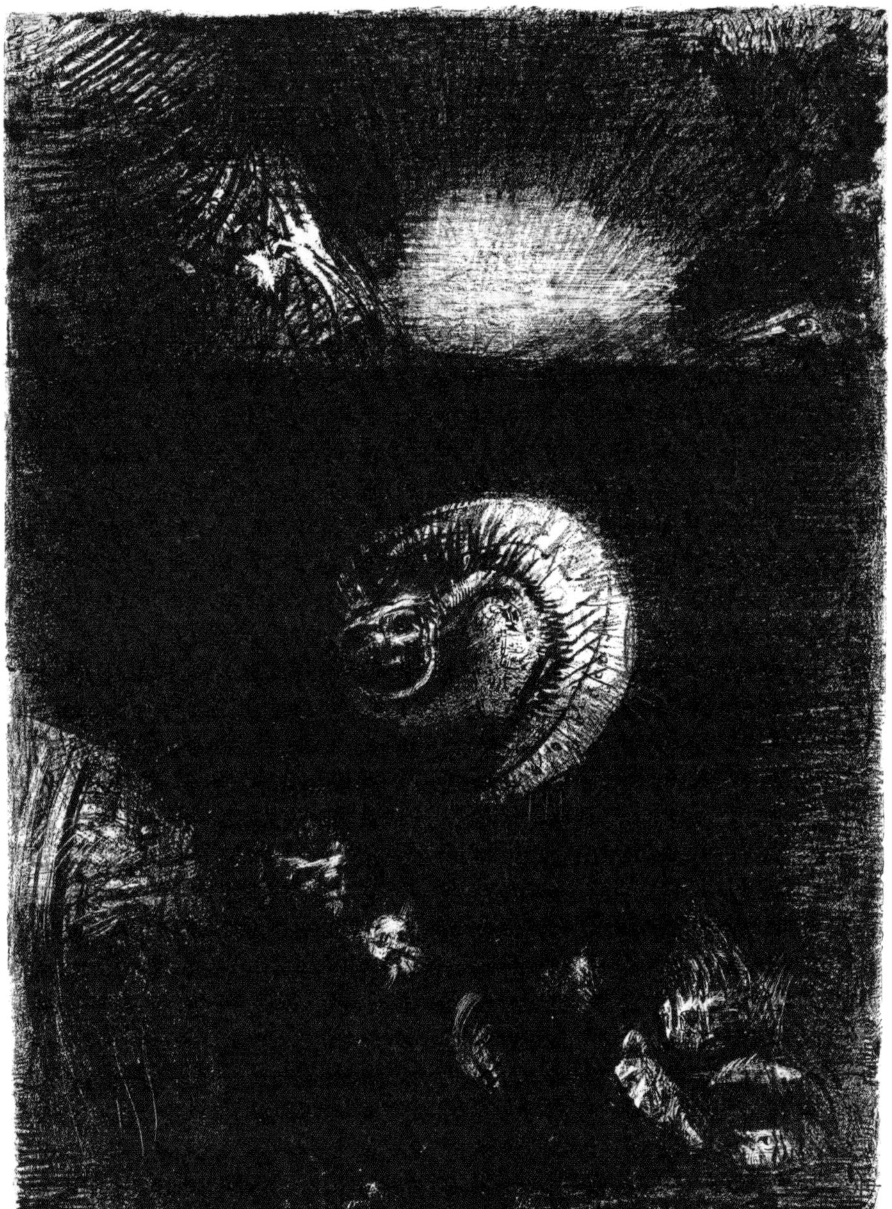

Pl. VIII.

Et toutes sortes de bêtes effroyables surgissent.

15
And All Manner of Frightful Creatures Arise, 1888
Plate VIII from the portfolio *Temptation of Saint Anthony*

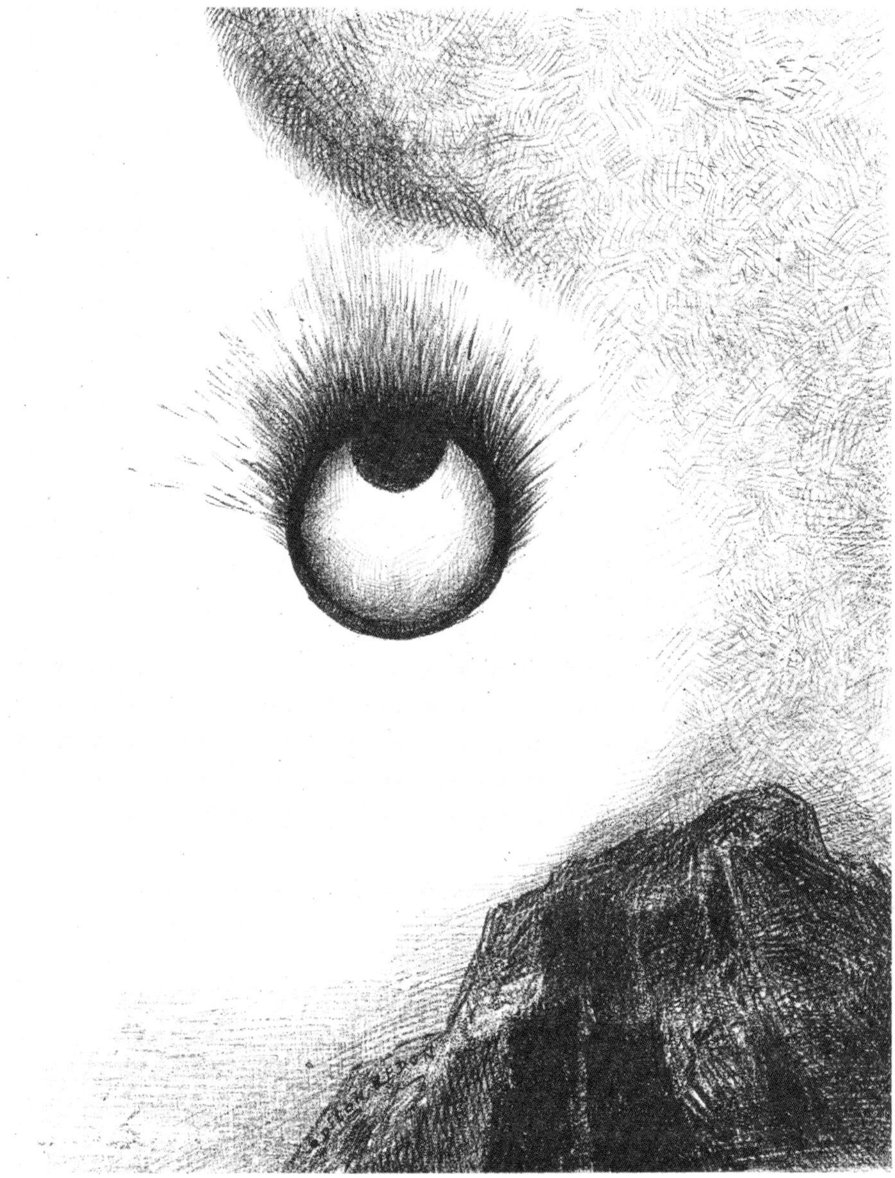

Pl. IX.

Partout des prunelles flamboient.

16
Everywhere Eyeballs Are Aflame, 1888
Plate IX from the portfolio *Temptation of Saint Anthony*

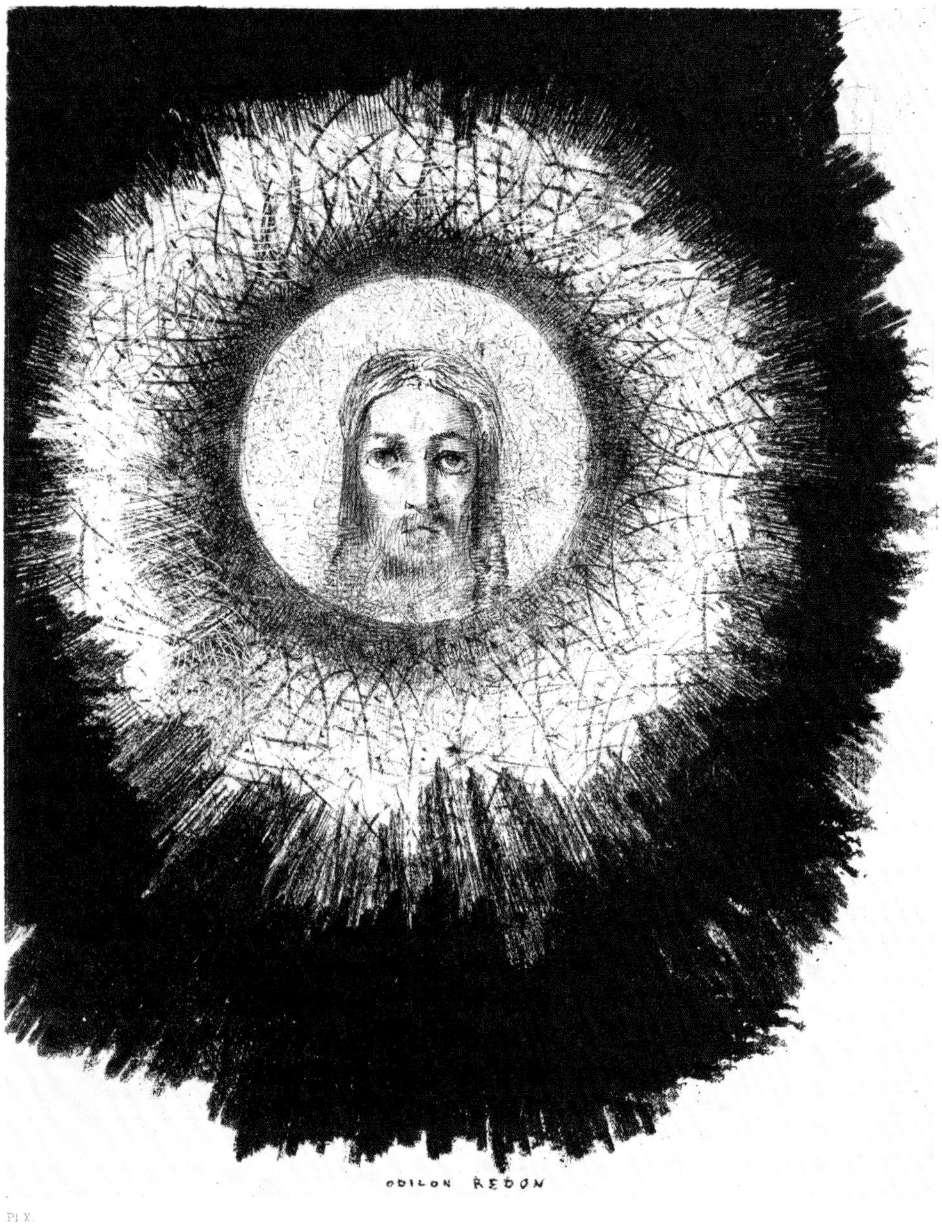

Pl X.

. . . . et dans le disque même du soleil, rayonne la face de Jésus-Christ.

17

And in the Very Disk of the Sun Shines the Face of Jesus Christ, 1888
Plate X from the portfolio *Temptation of Saint Anthony*

Dreams

Published in 1891, *Dreams* is a portfolio of six lithographs that Redon made in commemoration of his friend and mentor Armand Clavaud. A botanist and illustrator with interests in philosophy, art, and literature, Clavaud introduced Redon to new ways of seeing. His work on plant physiology, which was influenced by the findings of Charles Darwin, involved observations of the "infinitely small" through the lens of a microscope. The friendship informed Redon's interest in plants and his desire to capture that which is "at the edge of the imperceptible world." Later in life Redon would credit Clavaud with introducing him to not only modern evolutionary theory but also Hindu poetry, the Dutch philosopher Baruch Spinoza, and the writings of Edgar Allan Poe. Made shortly after Clavaud took his own life in 1890, this portfolio reflects the importance of their lasting relationship.

The six prints at first seem disconnected, evoking the strange and unexpected blend of imagery that arises in a dreamscape. The face of Christ appears emblazoned on the Veil of Veronica (plate 19); a hooded figure holding a bow hovers in a floating orb (plate 20); a pilgrim on horseback gazes up toward a glowing light (plate 23). Although several of the subjects are drawn from biblical or mythological sources, the bizarre combination of motifs divests the images of their particular symbolism in pursuit of a more general representation of the spiritual. The poetic titles, inscribed on the bottom of the sheets, only add to the ambiguity.

Dreams demonstrates Redon's increasing command of the lithographic crayon, which he used to craft haunting and dynamic scenes from the contrast of black printer's ink on white paper. The varied prints are united by the dramatic representation of shadows and light, setting the figures in a transitional space between the earthly and celestial. Redon often used windows or portals in his work to create a distinction between what we perceive and an otherworldly space. The final work in the portfolio, simply titled *Day* (plate 24), depicts a view through a window from an unlit room. Outside this window, a flourishing tree is visible in the sunlit exterior—perhaps a glimpse of what the artist envisioned beyond this life for his friend Clavaud.

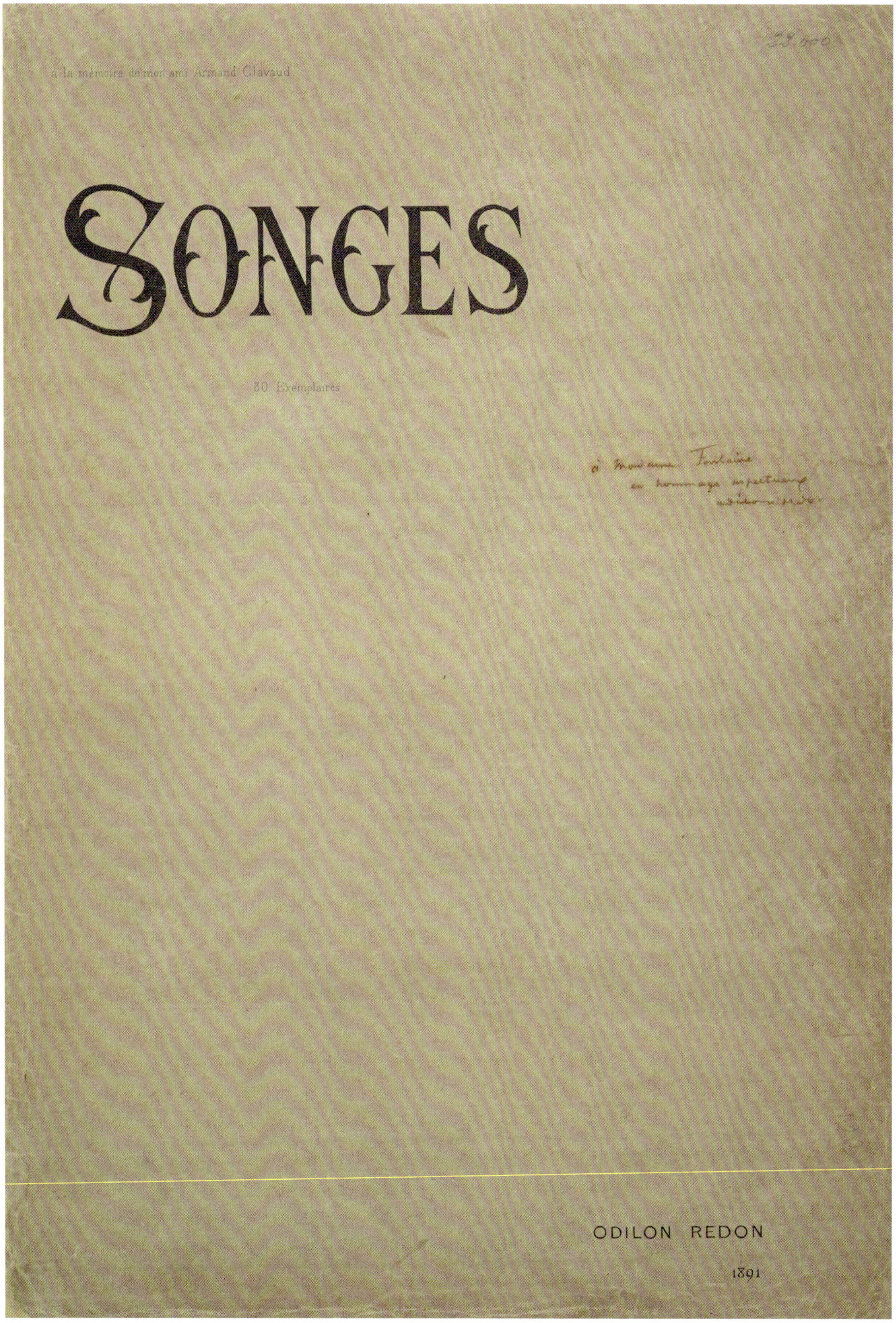

18
Cover of *Dreams*, 1891

pl.I

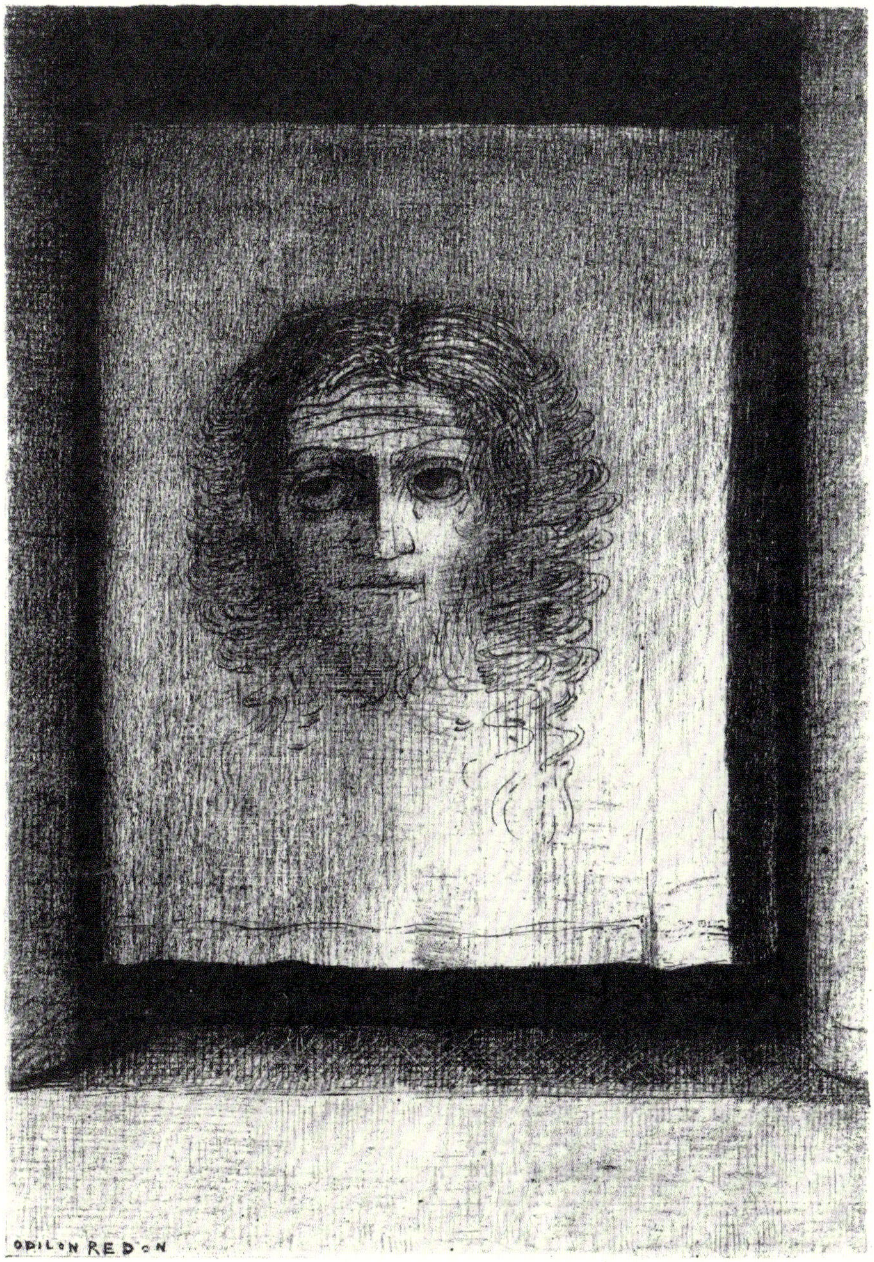

..............c'était un voile, une EMPREINTE..............

19
It Was a Veil, an Imprint, 1891
Plate I from the portfolio *Dreams*

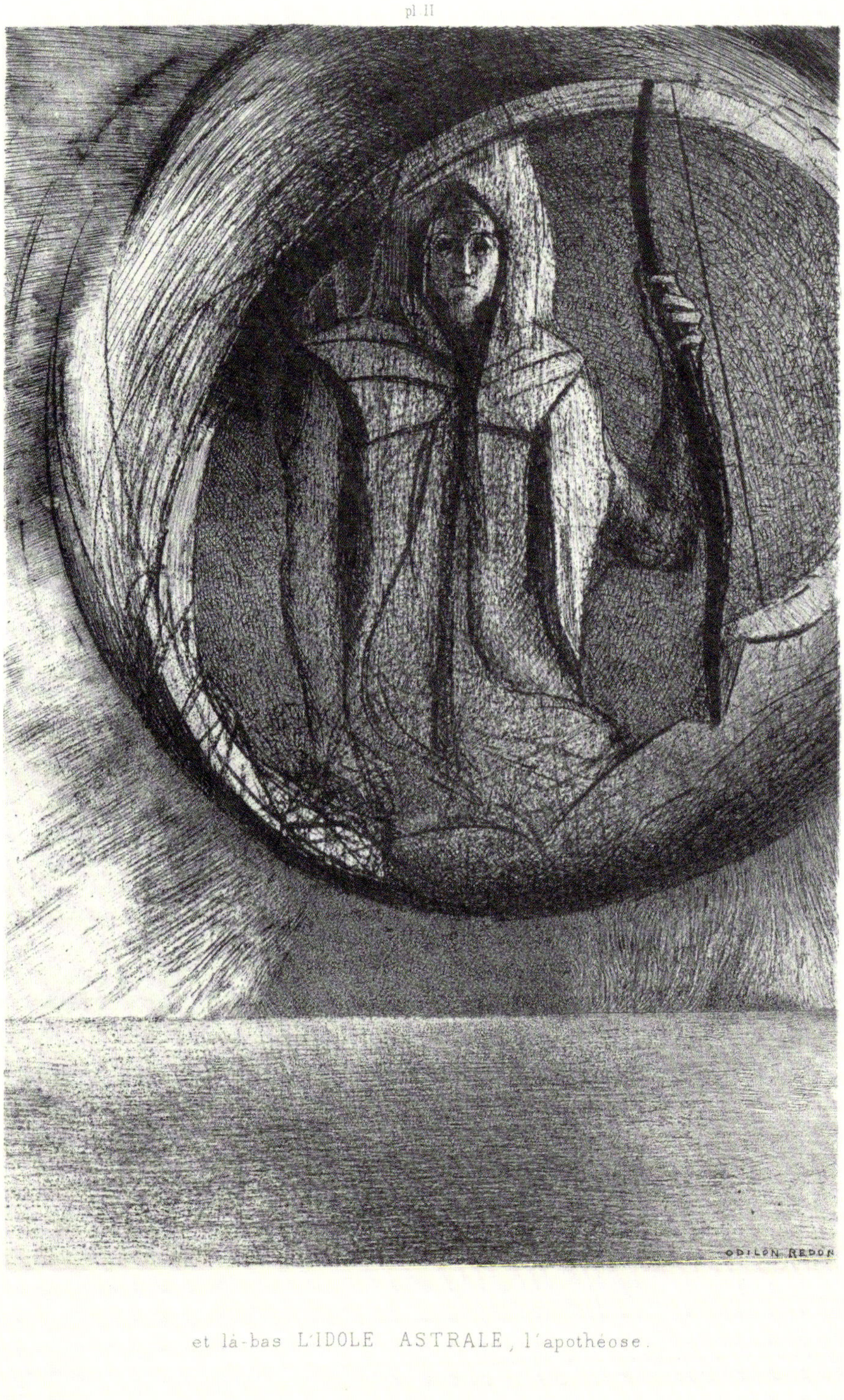

20
And Beyond, the Astral Idol, the Apotheosis, 1891
Plate II from the portfolio *Dreams*

pl. III

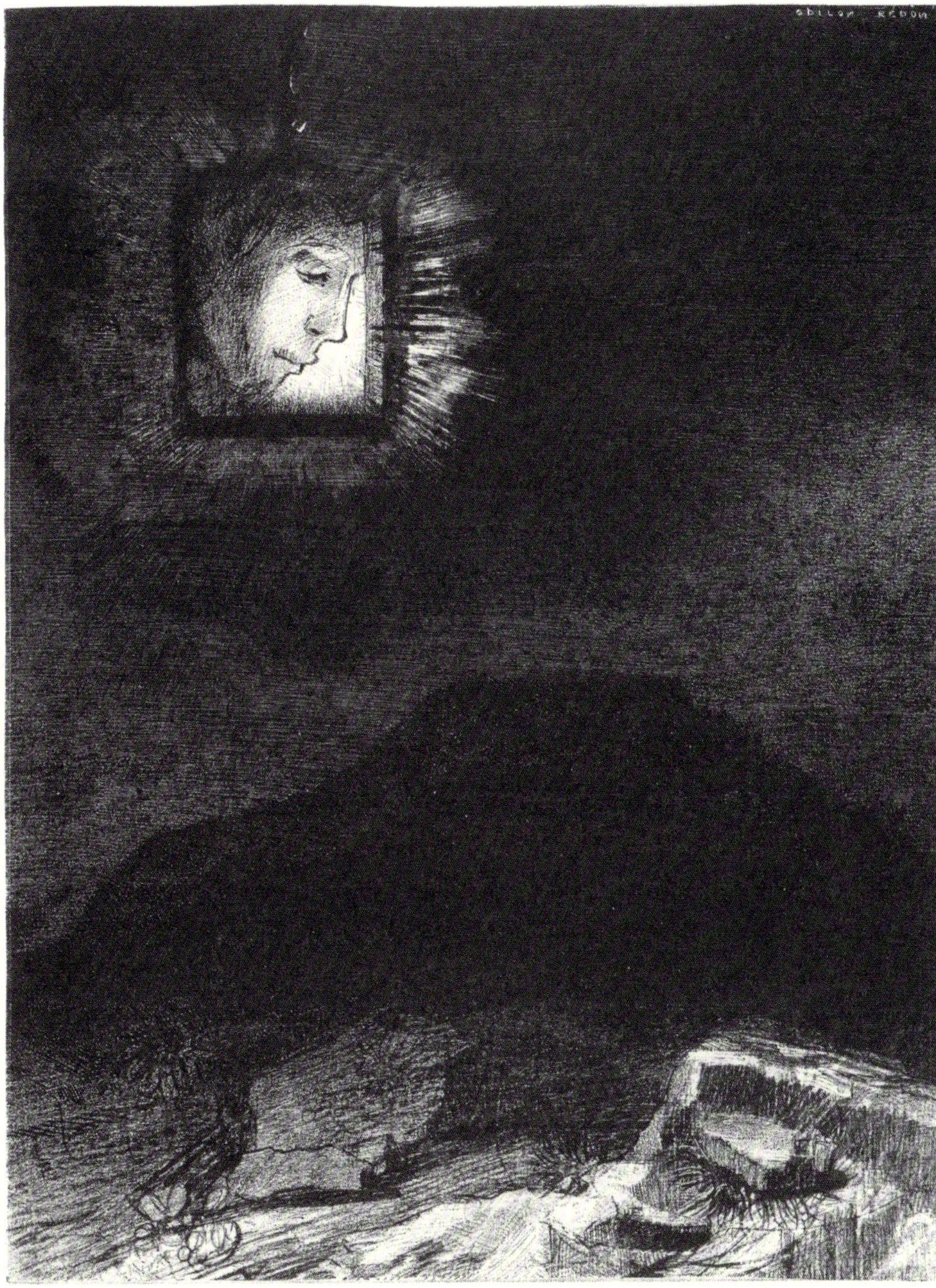

LUEUR PRÉCAIRE, une tête à l'infini suspendue.

21

Precarious Glimmering, a Head Suspended in Infinity, 1891
Plate III from the portfolio *Dreams*

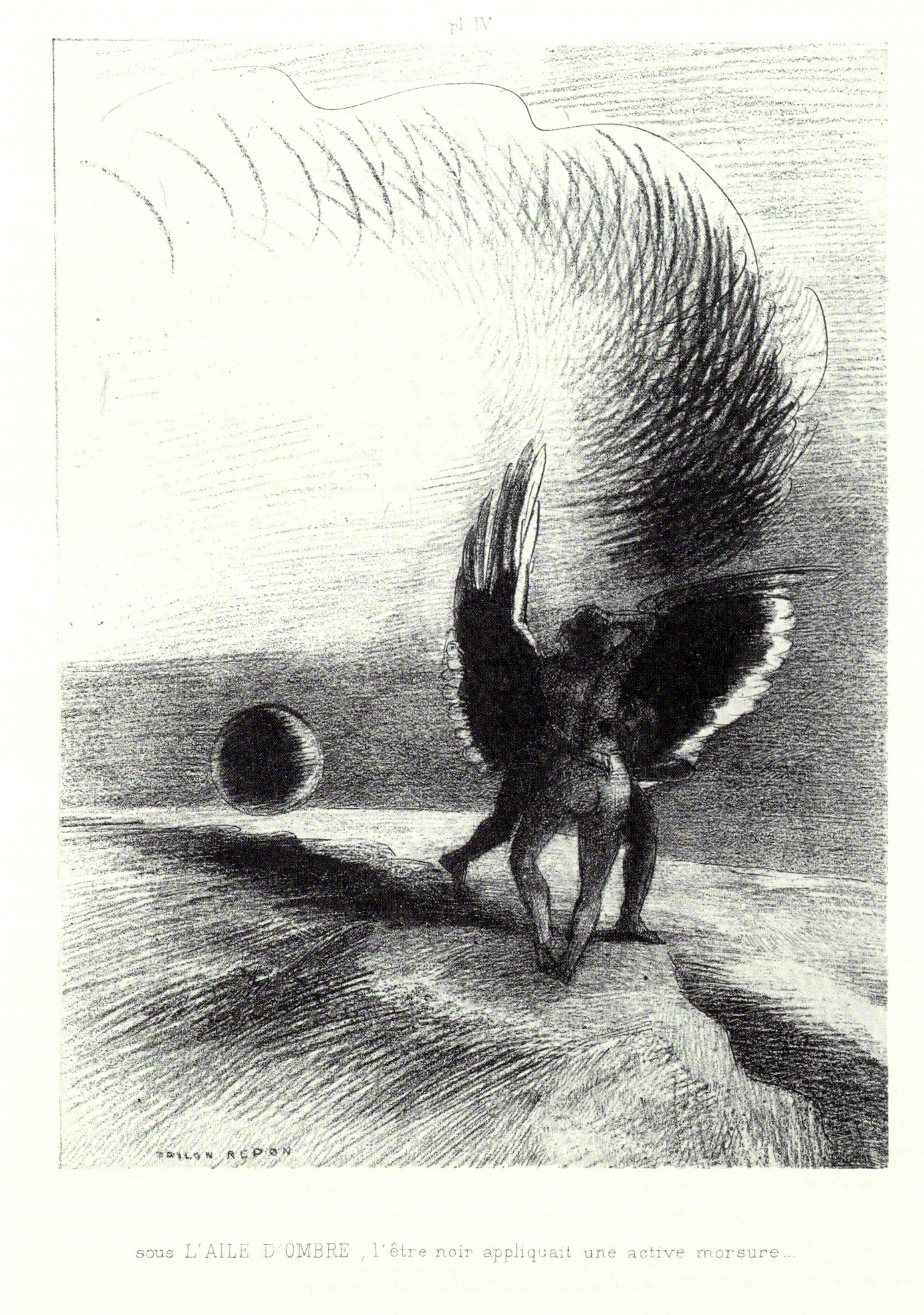

22
Beneath the Wing of Shadow the Black Creature Was Biting Energetically, 1891
Plate IV from the portfolio *Dreams*

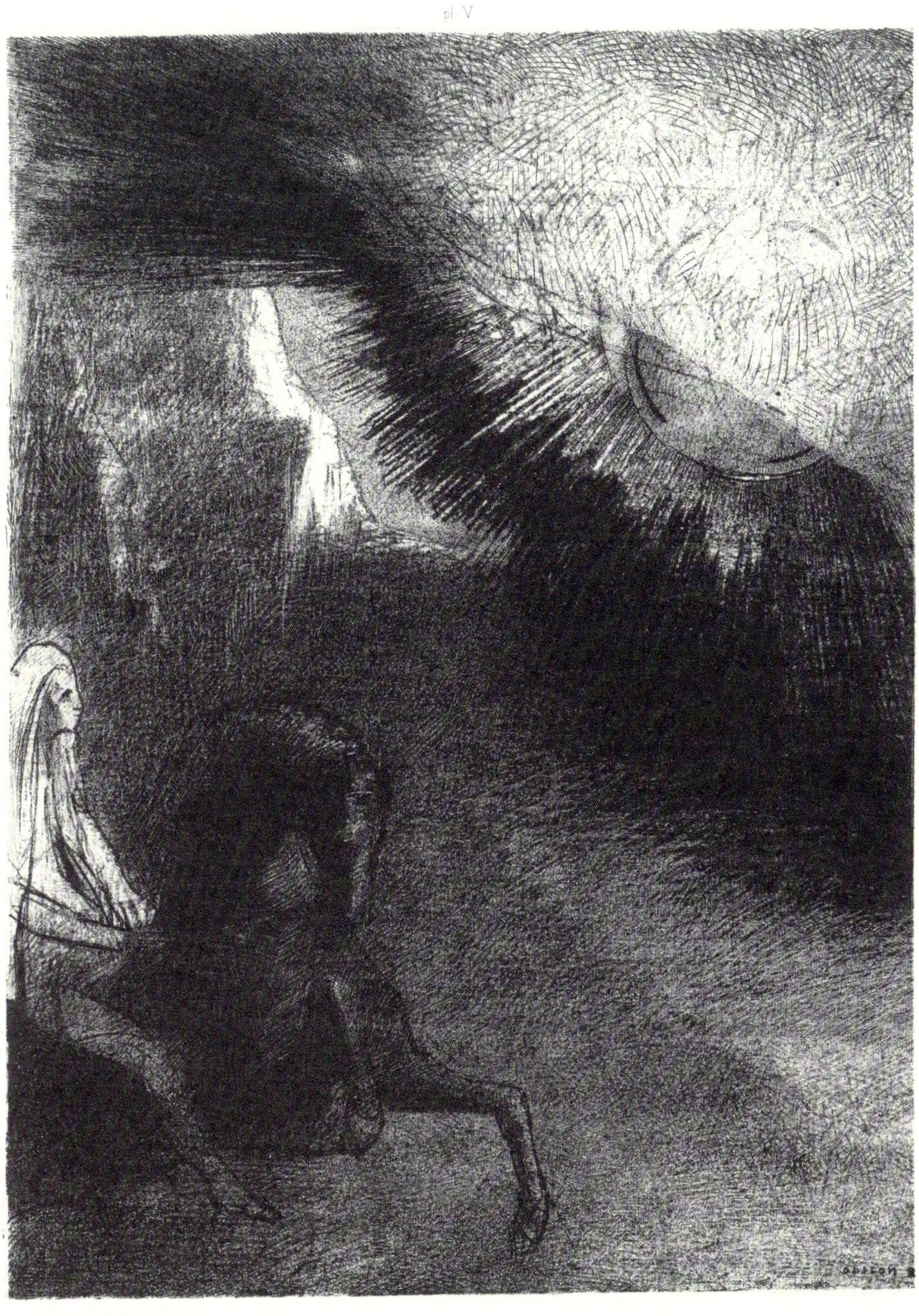

23
Pilgrim of the Sublunary World, 1891
Plate V from the portfolio *Dreams*

pl. VI

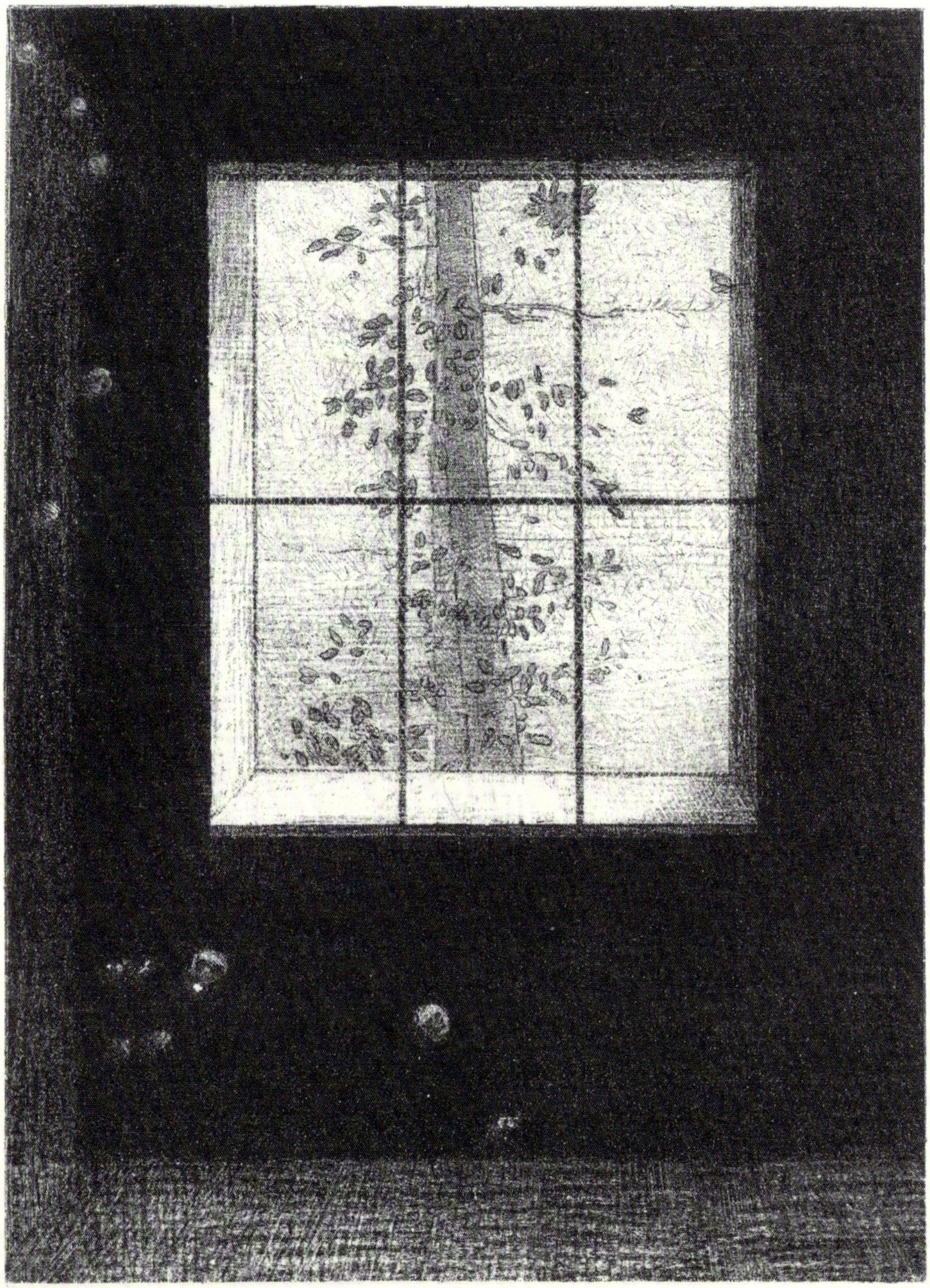

LE JOUR

24
Day, 1891
Plate VI from the portfolio *Dreams*

Apocalypse of Saint John

The last of Redon's eleven lithographic portfolios, *Apocalypse of Saint John*, depicts scenes from the final book of the Christian Bible, the Book of Revelation. Published in 1899 by the dealer Ambroise Vollard, the portfolio is the closest to traditional illustration of any of Redon's print series. The dramatic narrative, which is rife with symbolic imagery, relates to Saint John's vision of the apocalyptic events that culminate in the second coming of Jesus Christ. Redon was likely inspired by a celebrated series of fifteen woodcuts on the same theme by the German Renaissance printmaker Albrecht Dürer, whose work he admired. While Dürer took a realistic approach to interpreting the apocalyptic story, Redon found inspiration in the fantastical details of the narrative.

Each of the twelve lithographs in Redon's portfolio corresponds to a section of the biblical text, with quotations that follow a sequential order used as captions. Teeming with spectral figures and mysterious creatures, this apocalyptic story is well suited to Redon's visual vocabulary. Death, depicted as an animated skeleton, careens forward on horseback while wielding a long sword (plate 28). Elsewhere, an angel flies down from heaven, swathed in darkness and grasping a long chain (plate 33). While some of the quotations are more liberally interpreted, each print reflects a narrative moment in the biblical story. Despite the less ambiguous nature of the images, Redon still imbued his scenes with mystery and drama through the skillful employment of lithographic techniques. In *And the Angel Took the Censer* (plate 29), for example, the soft smoke that billows around the figure is produced through layers of texture and tone against the bare white sheet.

Apocalypse of Saint John represents the end of Redon's decades-long engagement with lithography, although he continued to make occasional single prints. The directness of the compositions, which conclude with a simple portrait of Saint John in profile (plate 37), portends the artist's transition to the more straightforward representations of figures and nature he produced in the last decades of his life.

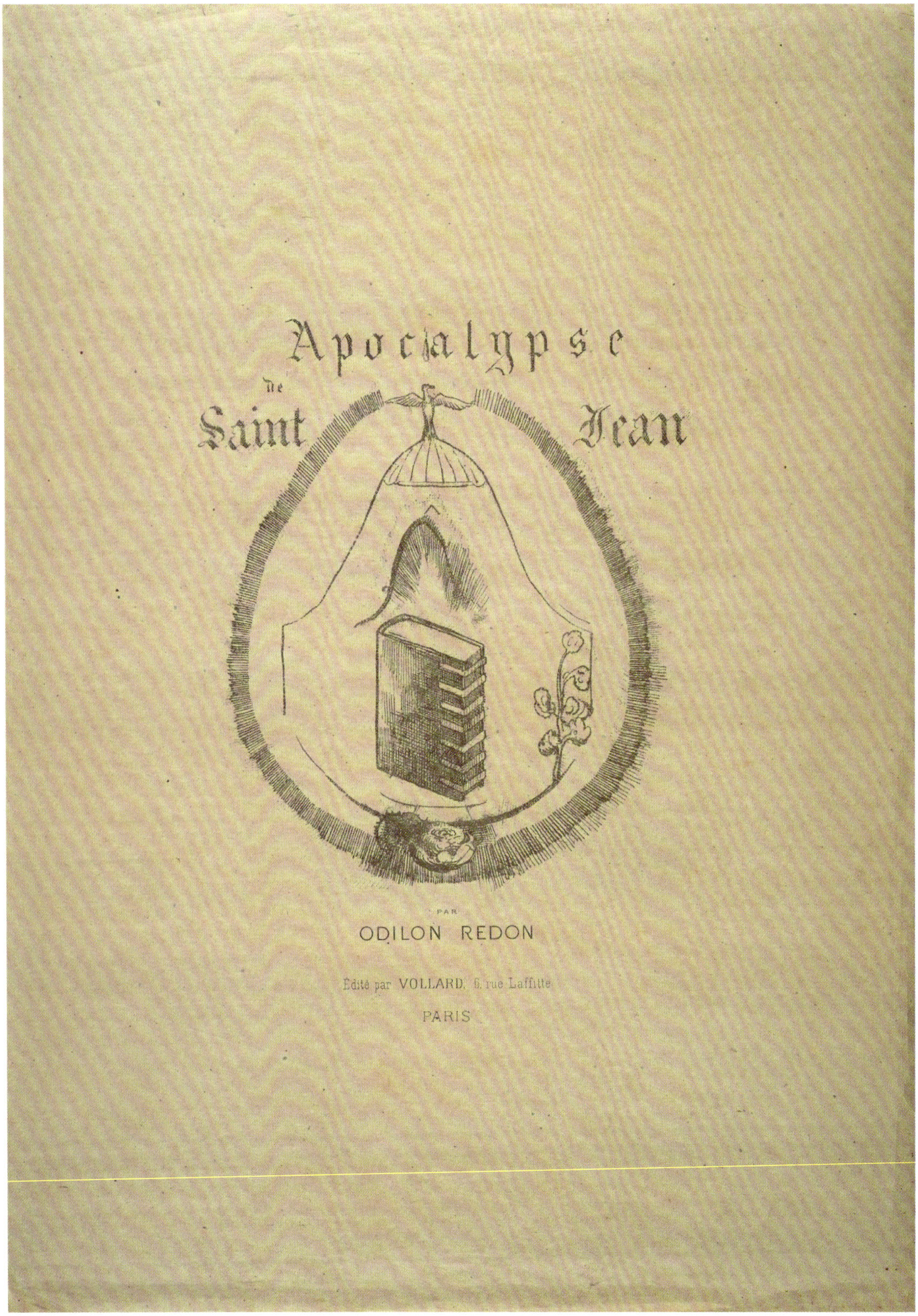

25
Cover of *Apocalypse of Saint John*, 1899

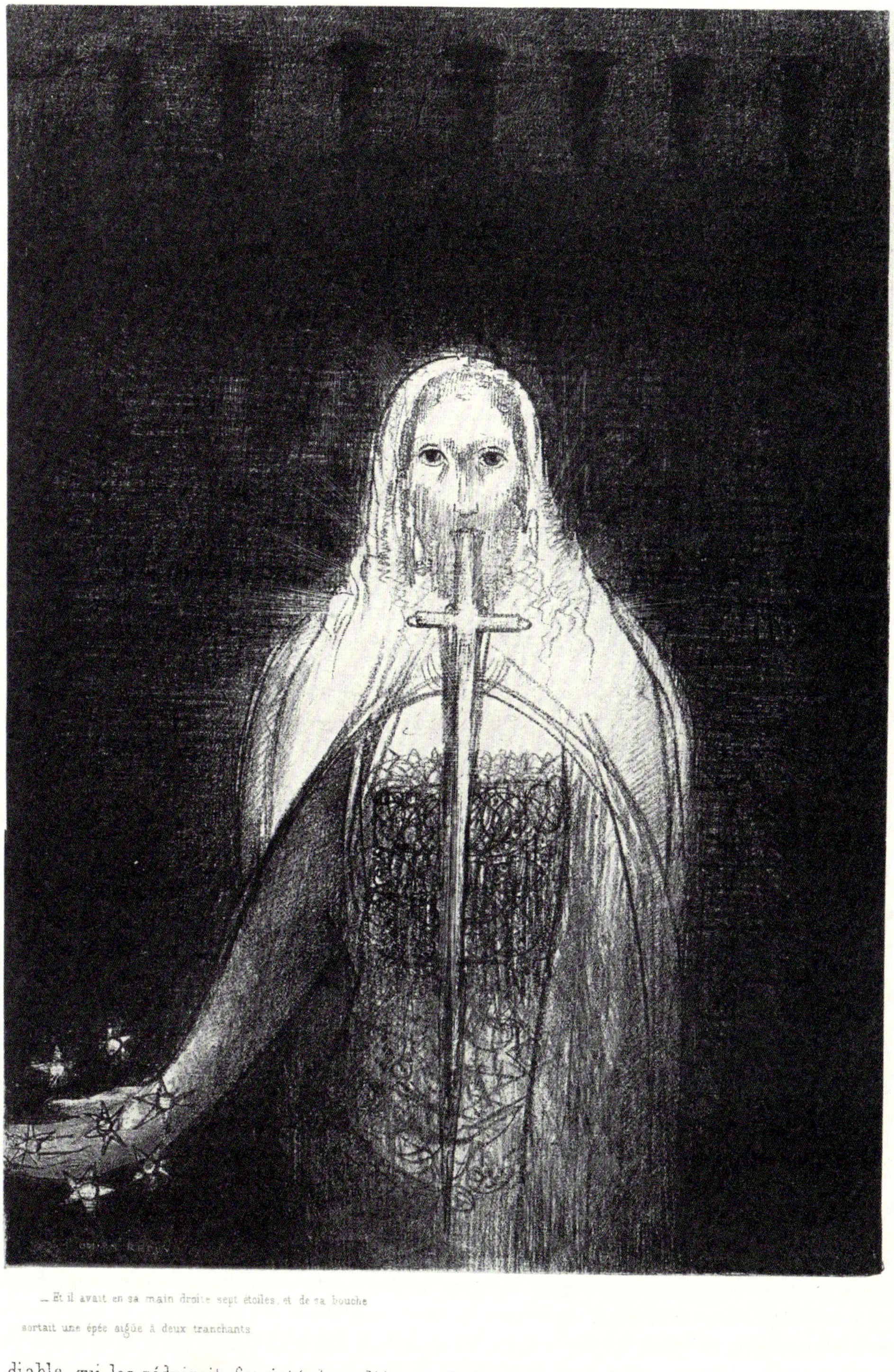

— Et il avait en sa main droite sept étoiles, et de sa bouche
sortait une épée aigüe à deux tranchants

— Et le diable qui les séduisait, fut jeté dans l'étang de feu et de soufre,

26
And He Had in His Right Hand Seven Stars; and Out of His Mouth Went a Sharp Two-Edged Sword, 1899
Plate I from the portfolio *Apocalypse of Saint John*

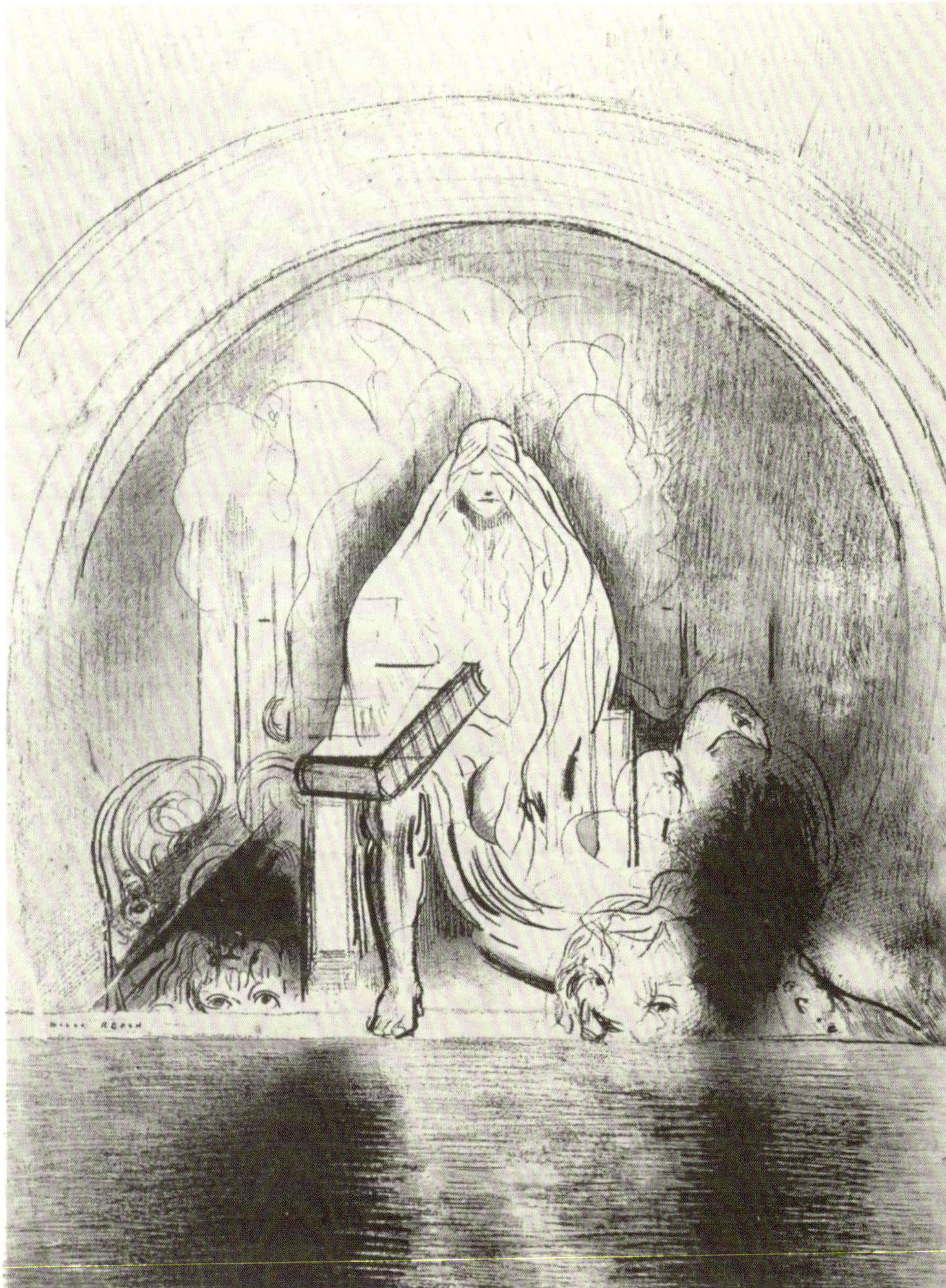

— Puis je vis dans la main droite de celui qui était assis sur le trône
un livre écrit dedans et dehors, scellé de sept sceaux

27

And I Saw in the Right Hand of Him That Sat on the Throne a Book Written Within and on the Backside, Sealed with Seven Seals, 1899

Plate II from the portfolio *Apocalypse of Saint John*

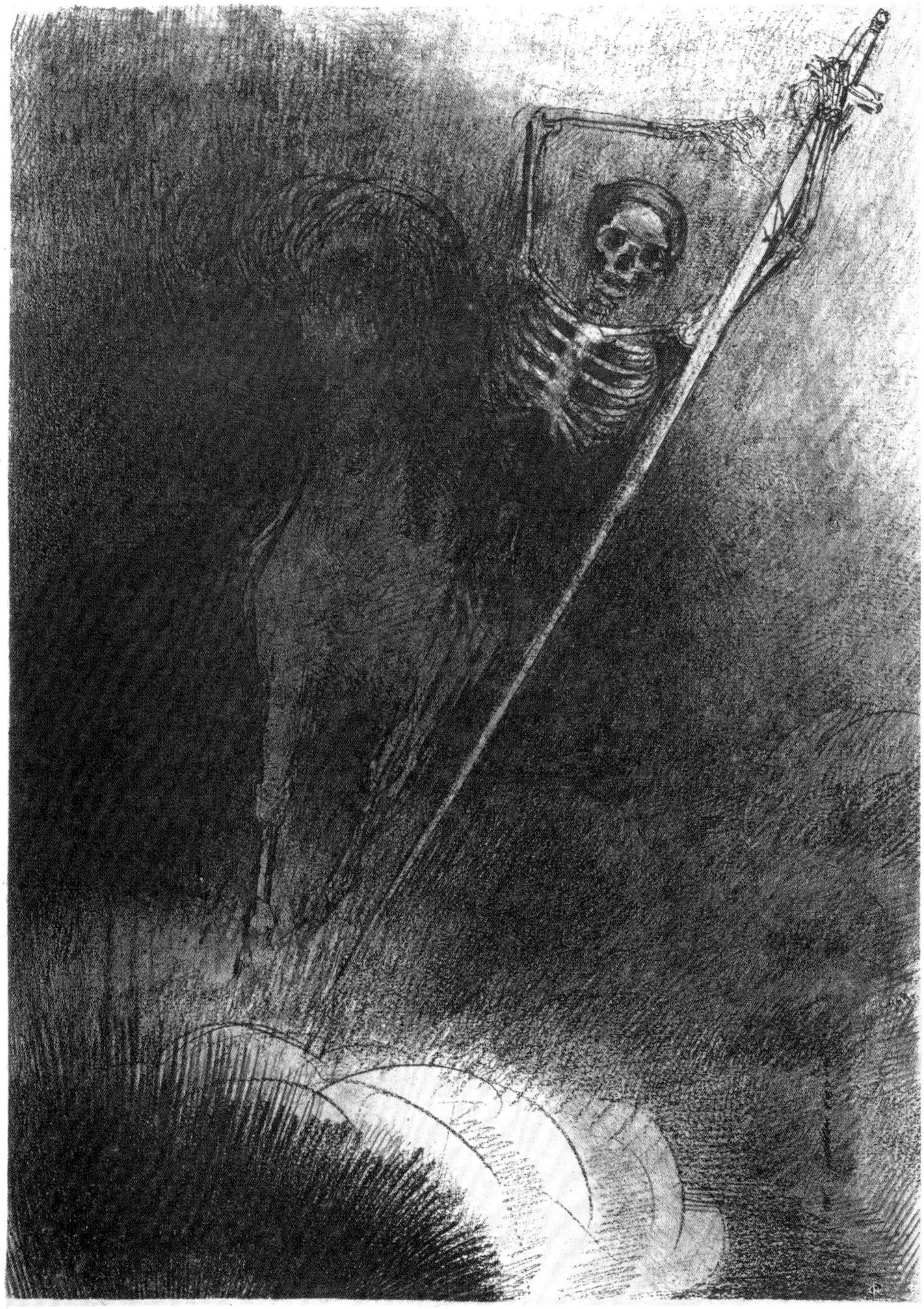

...... et celui qui était monté dessus se nommait la Mort,

28

And His Name That Sat on Him Was Death, 1899
Plate III from the portfolio *Apocalypse of Saint John*

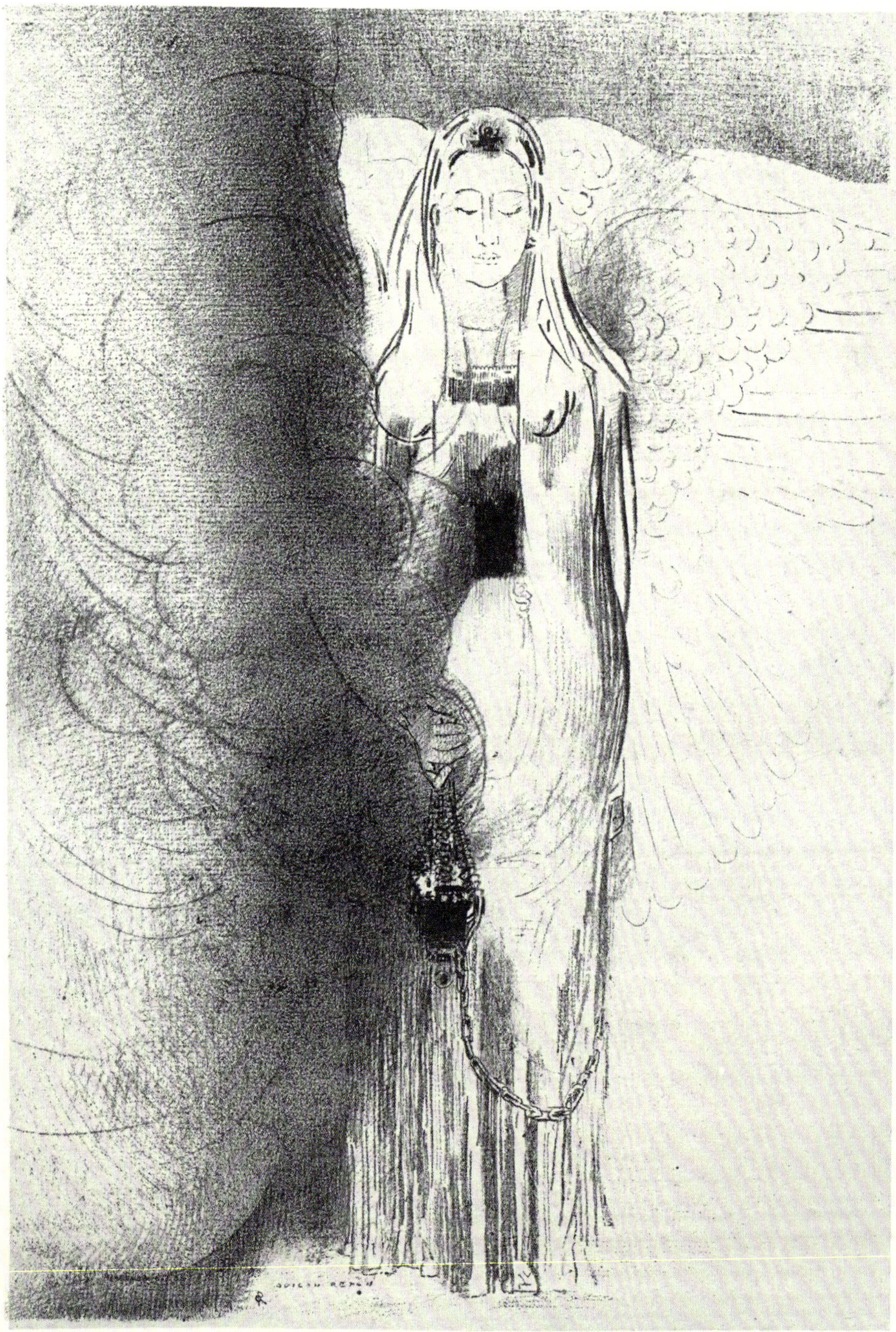

Puis l'ange prit l'encensoir

29
And the Angel Took the Censer, 1899
Plate IV from the portfolio *Apocalypse of Saint John*

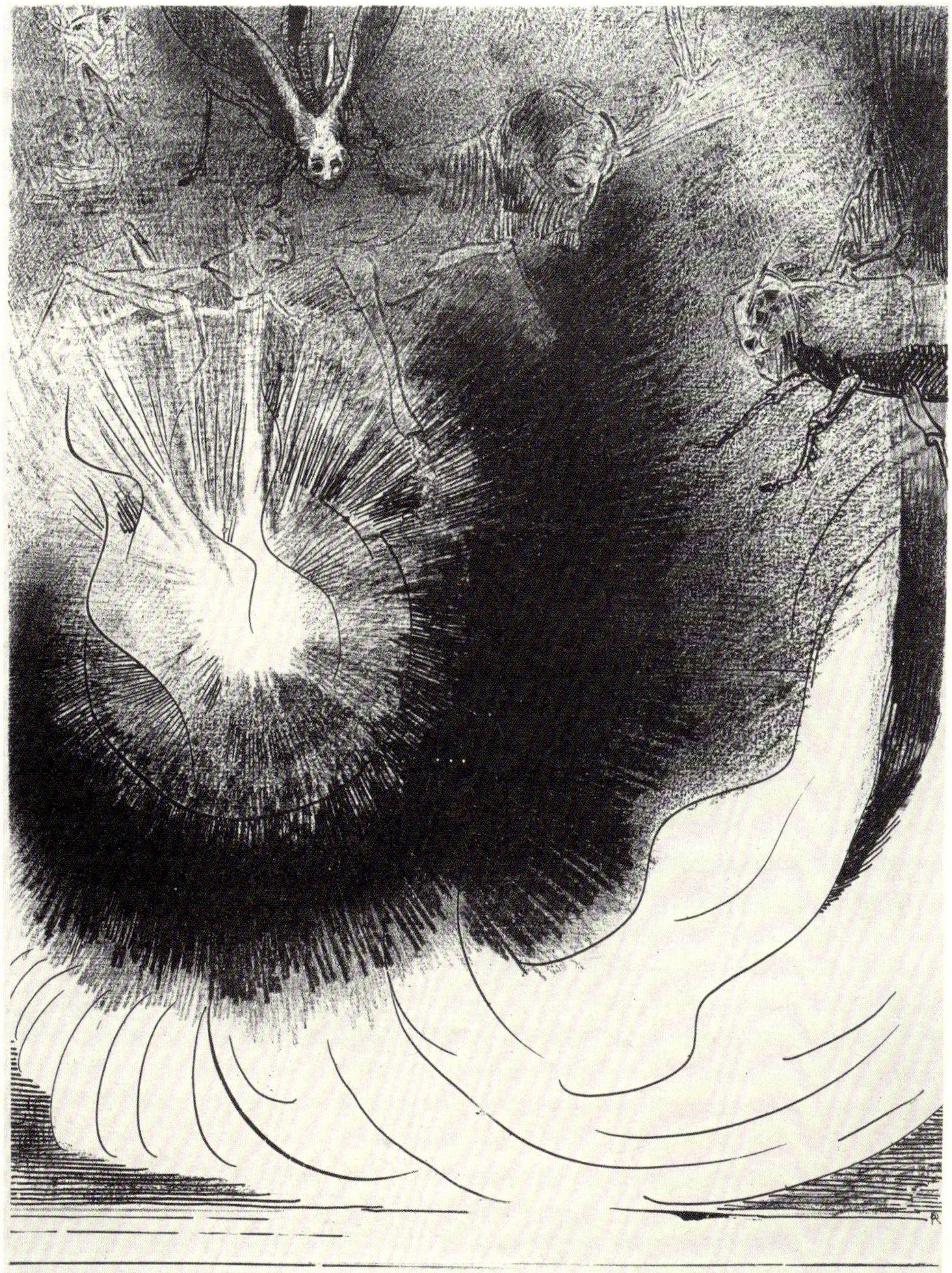

30

And There Fell a Great Star from Heaven, Burning as It Were a Lamp, 1899
Plate V from the portfolio *Apocalypse of Saint John*

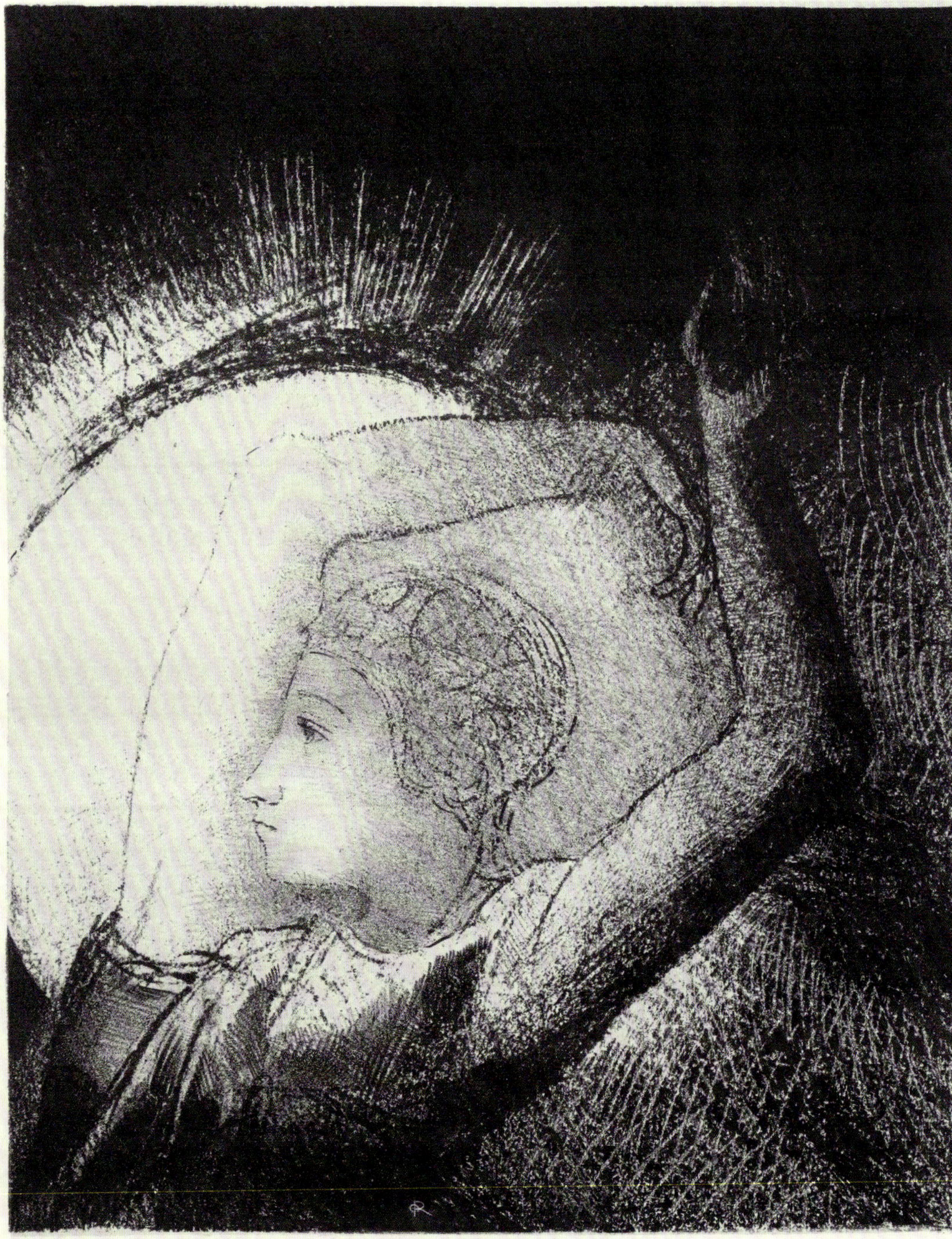

..... une femme revêtue du Soleil,

31
A Woman Clothed with the Sun, 1899
Plate VI from the portfolio *Apocalypse of Saint John*

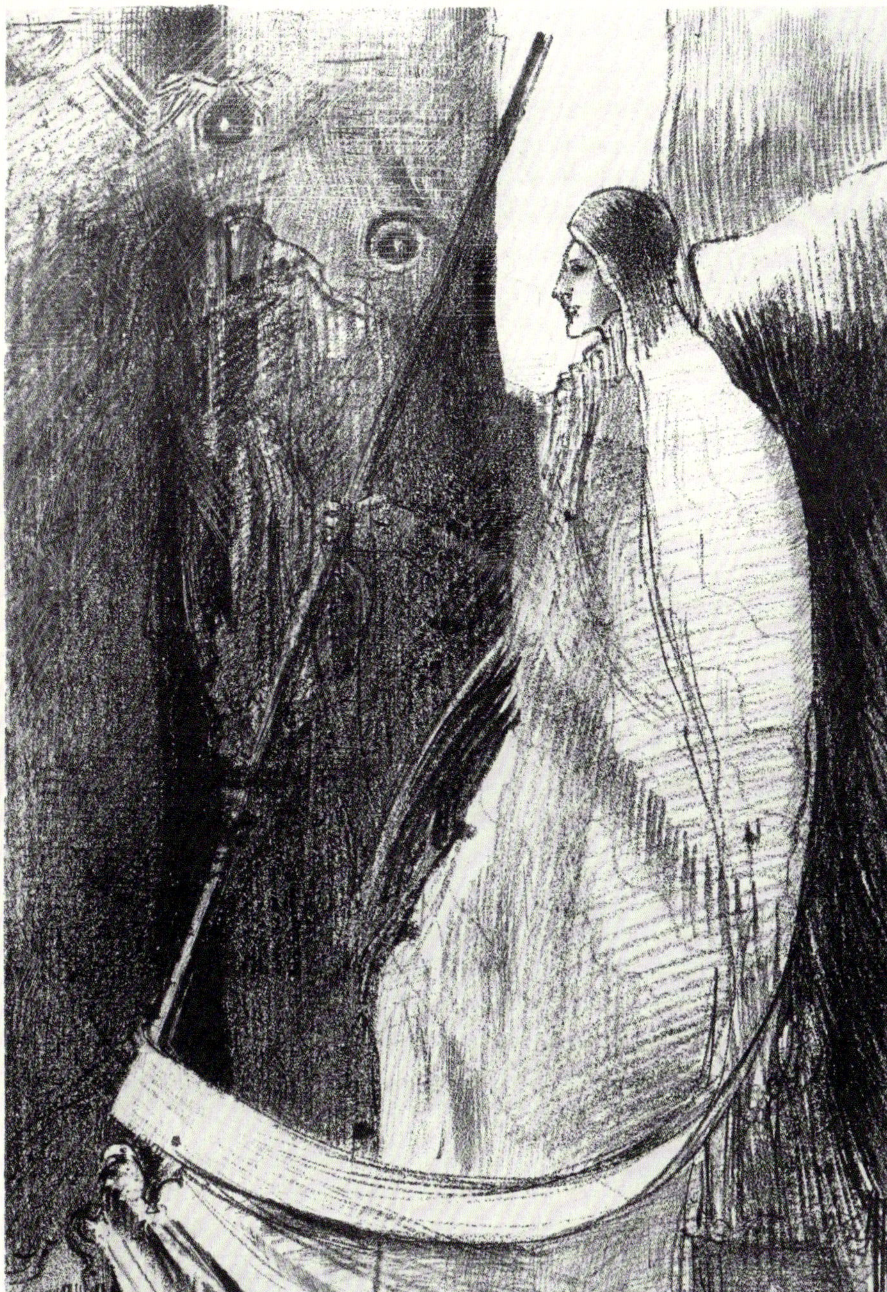

Et un autre ange sortit du temple qui est au ciel, ayant lui aussi une faucille tranchante.

32

And Another Angel Came Out of the Temple Which Is in Heaven, and He Also Having a Sharp Sickle, 1899
Plate VII from the portfolio *Apocalypse of Saint John*

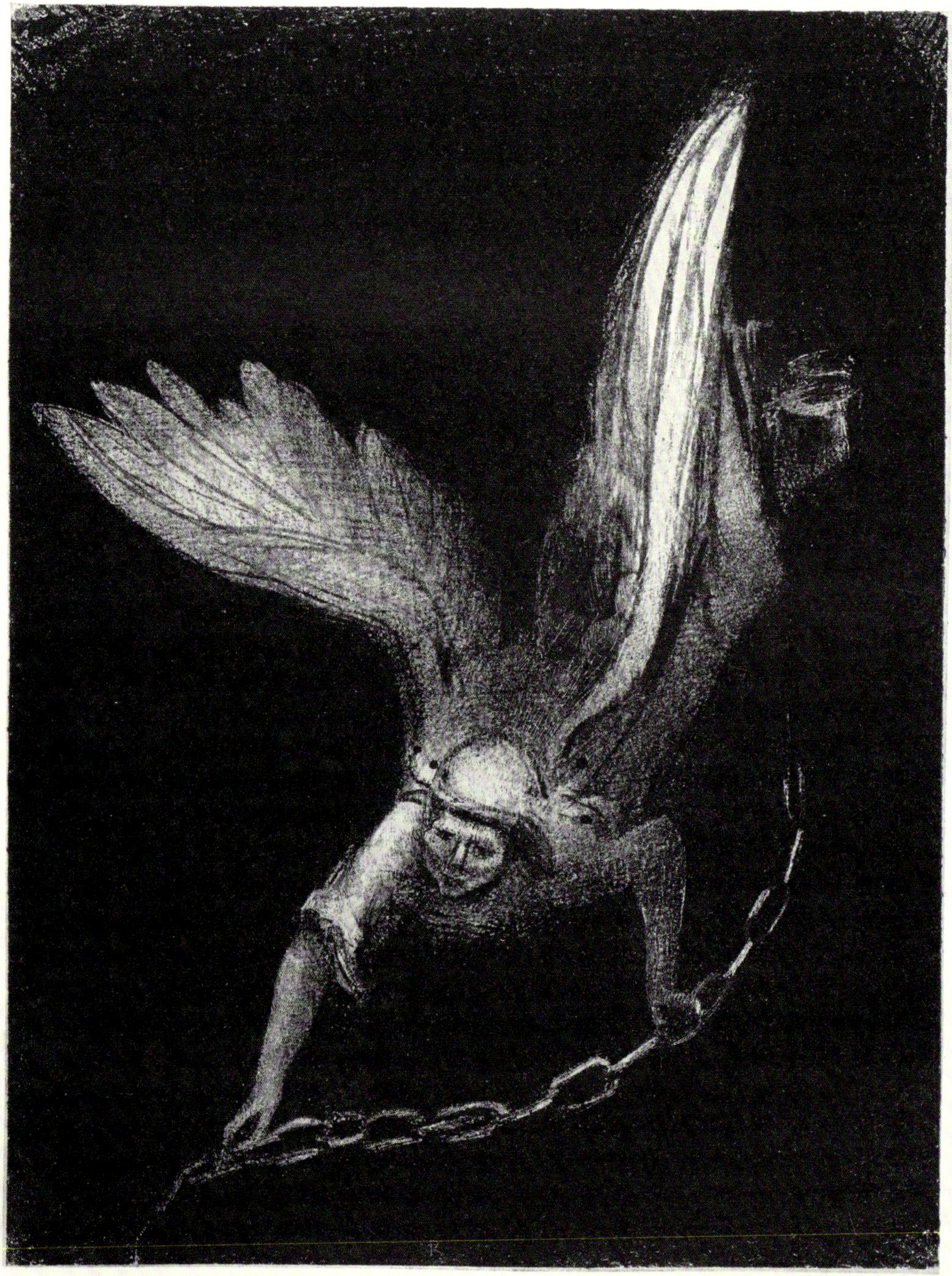

Après cela, je vis descendre du ciel un ange qui avait la clef de l'abîme, et une grande chaîne en sa main ;

33

And I Saw an Angel Coming Down from Heaven, Having the Key of the Bottomless Pit and a Great Chain in His Hand, 1899
Plate VIII from the portfolio *Apocalypse of Saint John*

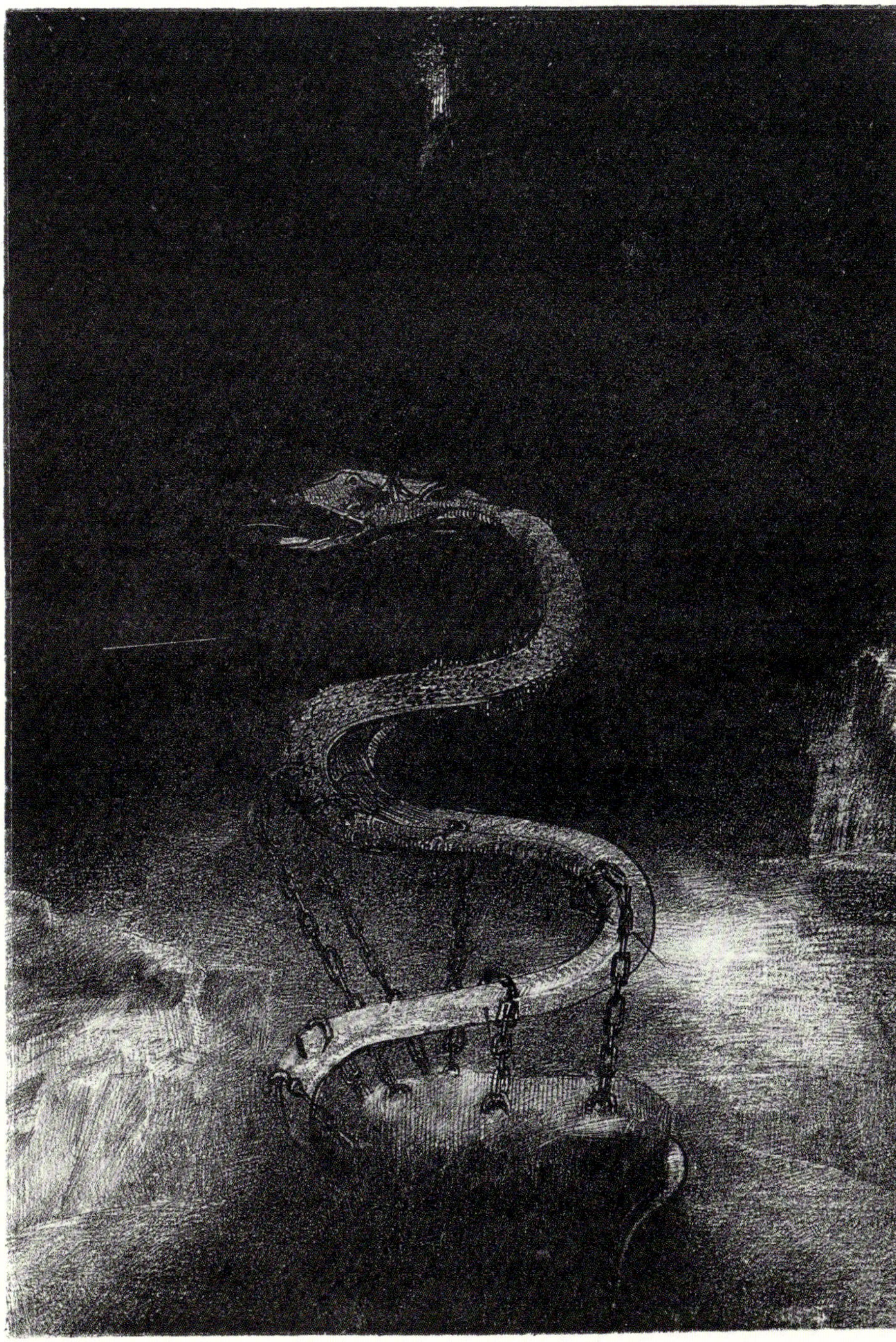

….. et le lia pour mille ans,

34
And Bound Him a Thousand Years, 1899
Plate IX from the portfolio *Apocalypse of Saint John*

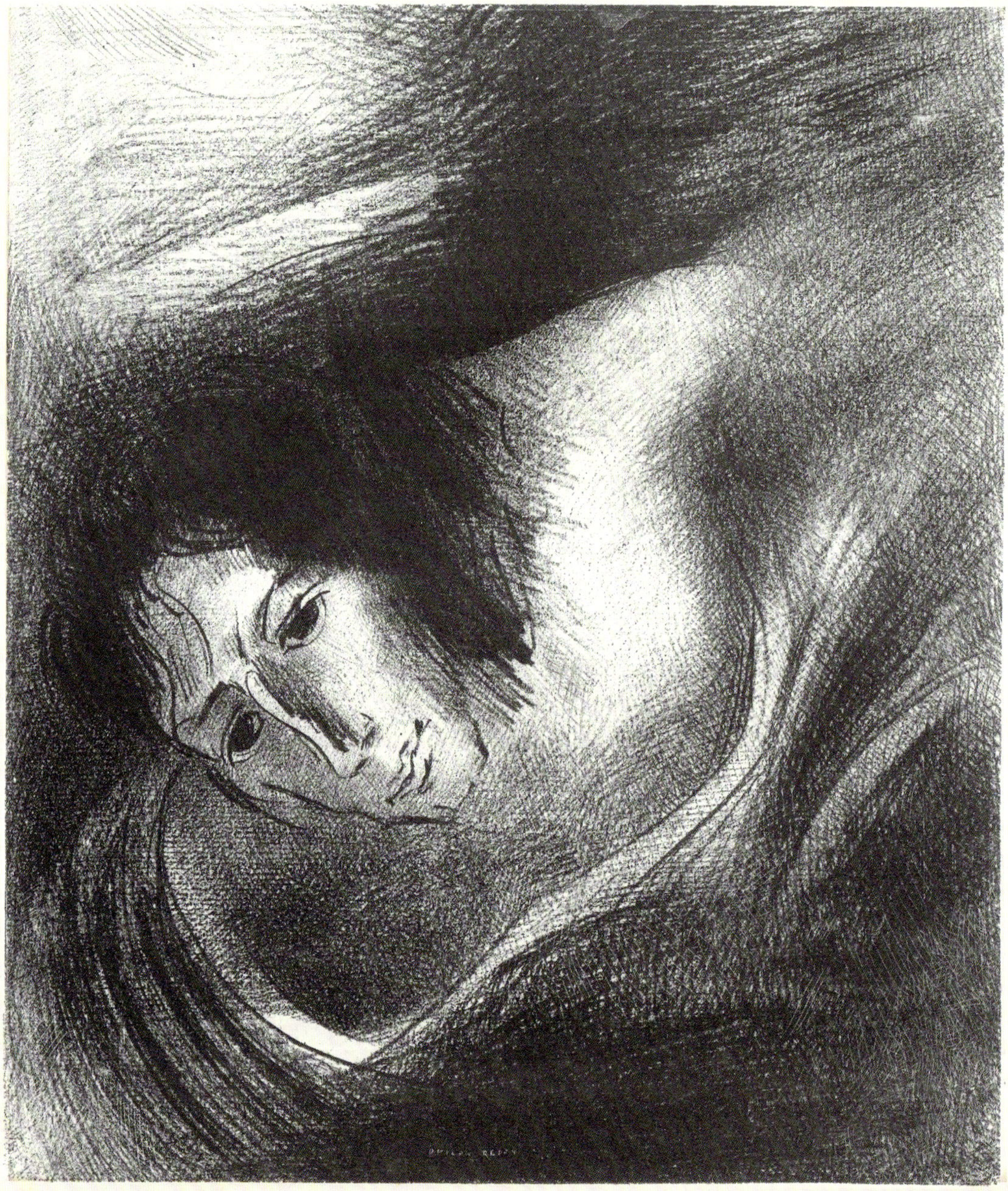

... Et le diable qui les séduisait, fut jeté dans l'étang de feu et de soufre,
où est la bête et le faux prophète;

35

And the Devil That Deceived Them Was Cast into the Lake Fire and Brimstone, Where the Beast and the False Prophet Are, 1899
Plate X from the portfolio *Apocalypse of Saint John*

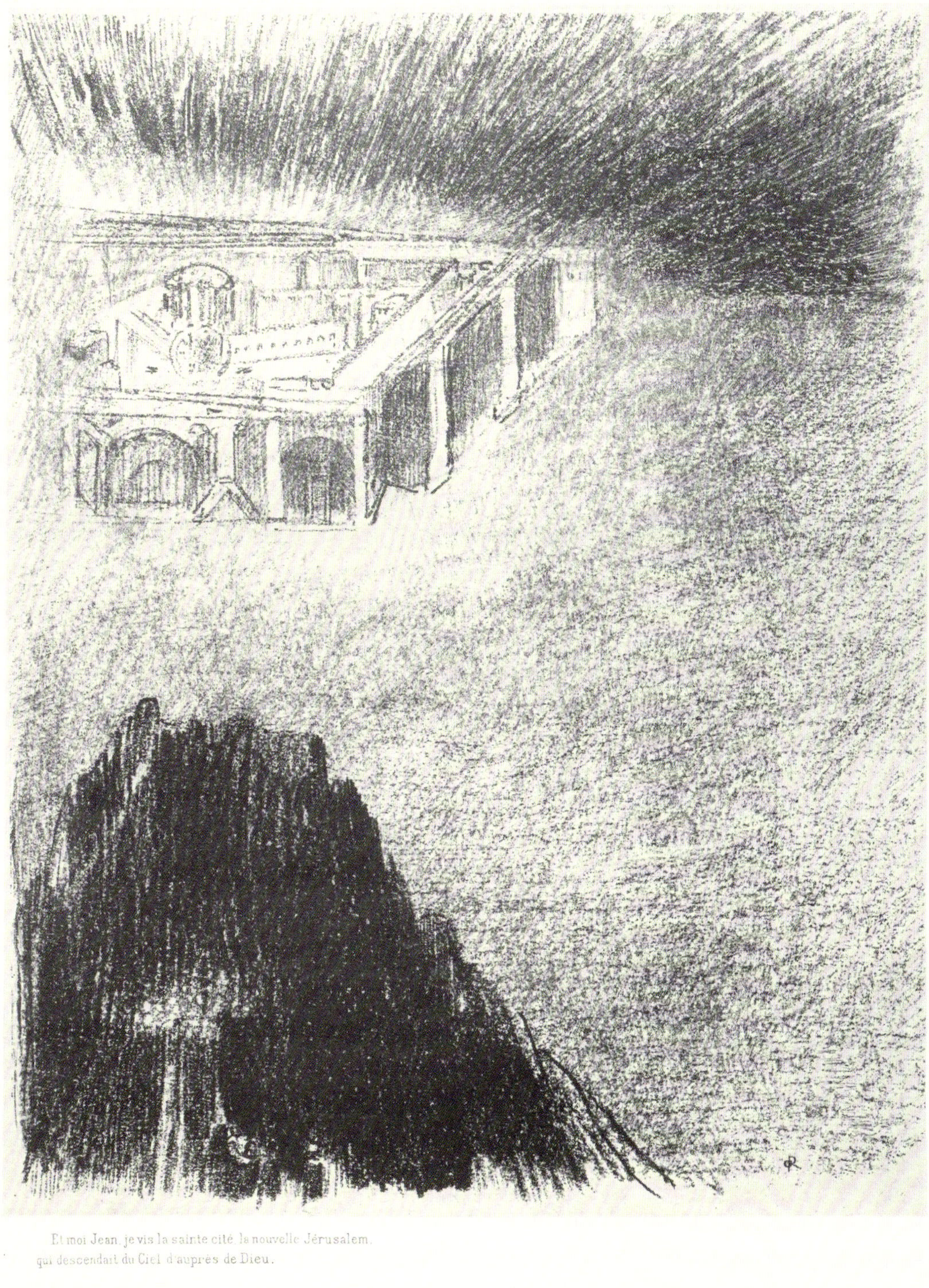

Et moi Jean, je vis la sainte cité, la nouvelle Jérusalem,
qui descendait du Ciel d'auprès de Dieu.

36

And I, John, Saw the Holy City, New Jerusalem, Coming Down from God and Out of Heaven, 1899
Plate XI from the portfolio *Apocalypse of Saint John*

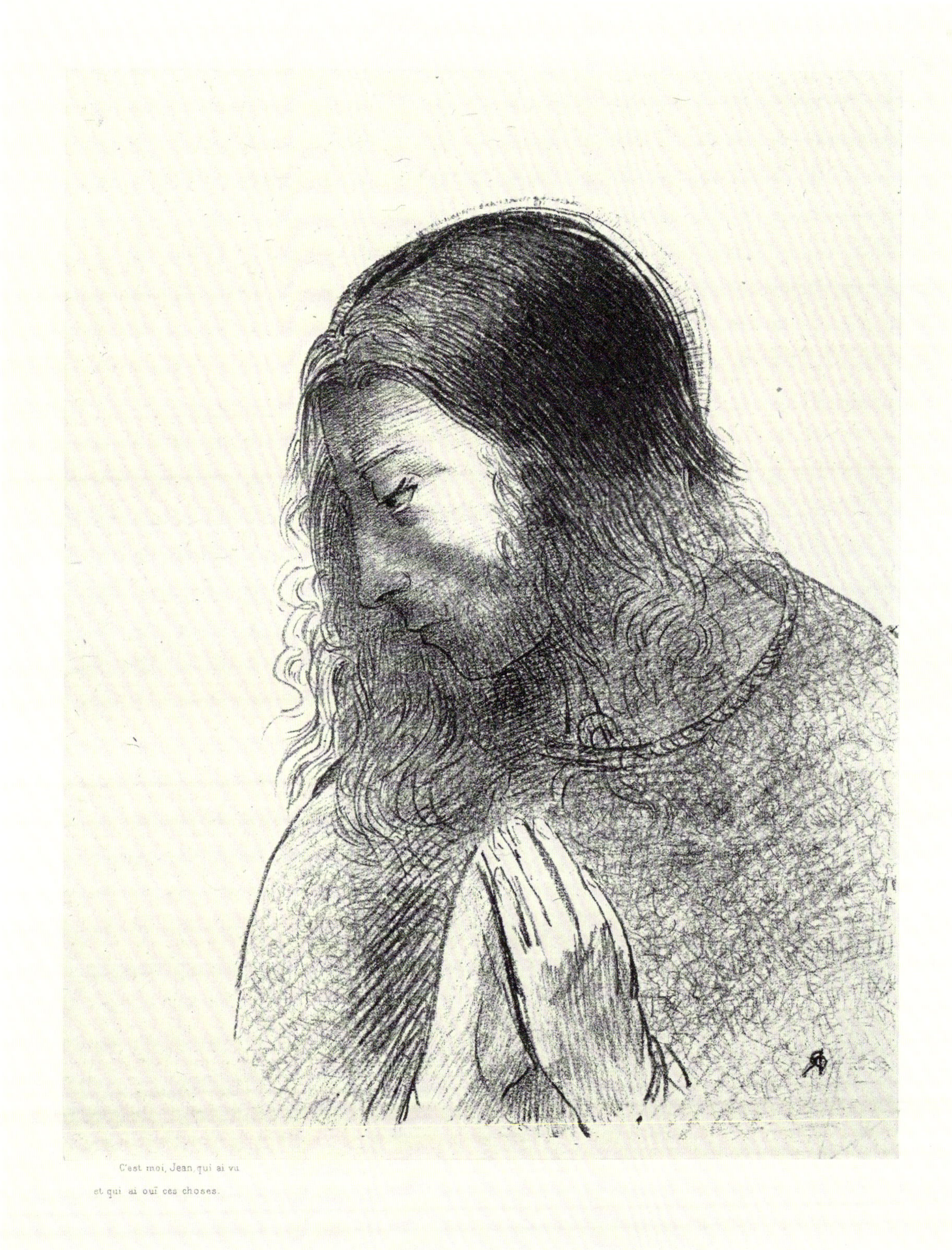

37
And I, John, Saw These Things, and Heard Them, 1899
Plate XII from the portfolio *Apocalypse of Saint John*

Color

In 1886 Redon appeared as a surprising participant in the eighth and final Impressionist exhibition in Paris. While the exhibition included an array of artists working in diverse styles, Redon stood out with his shadowy and macabre *noirs*. His fifteen moody charcoal drawings were hung in a hallway, separated from the brightly hued landscapes by artists like Camille Pissarro and Berthe Morisot. A decade later, Redon took an even more unexpected turn when he largely abandoned the black media he had become known for to create his own drawings, paintings, and prints in vibrant color.

Throughout his early career, Redon had used color selectively, including making small additions of watercolor and color pastel to his charcoal drawings. On frequent visits to his childhood home of Peyrelebade, he made light, sun-dappled oil studies of the surrounding landscape (see fig. 13). Yet this remained a minor and largely private aspect of his artistic practice until the 1890s, when he fully embraced bold, jewel-like tones as his primary means of expression. The luminous and often nonnaturalistic hues of his color pastels and oil paintings served to enhance the surreal and mystical aspects of his imagery. He even briefly experimented with color lithography, culminating in *Beatrice* (plate 41), an ethereal profile made in a full range of muted tones.

Redon's transition to color provided a fruitful means of expanding his imaginative vision. He found innovative ways to reconsider favored motifs, such as the severed heads of John the Baptist and Orpheus (plates 38, 44). At the same time, he explored original compositions that better fit with his new media, including portraits and floral still lifes. The bright colors and less ambiguous subject matter made these works popular with a broader group of collectors and offered Redon renewed commercial success. The radiant combination of hues, however, added an other-worldly quality even to these seemingly conventional compositions (plates 42, 43). By 1900 Redon fully defined himself by this vivid palette, holding a solo exhibition at the dealer Paul Durand-Ruel's gallery in Paris devoted entirely to his works in color, including the chromatic pastel of Orpheus.

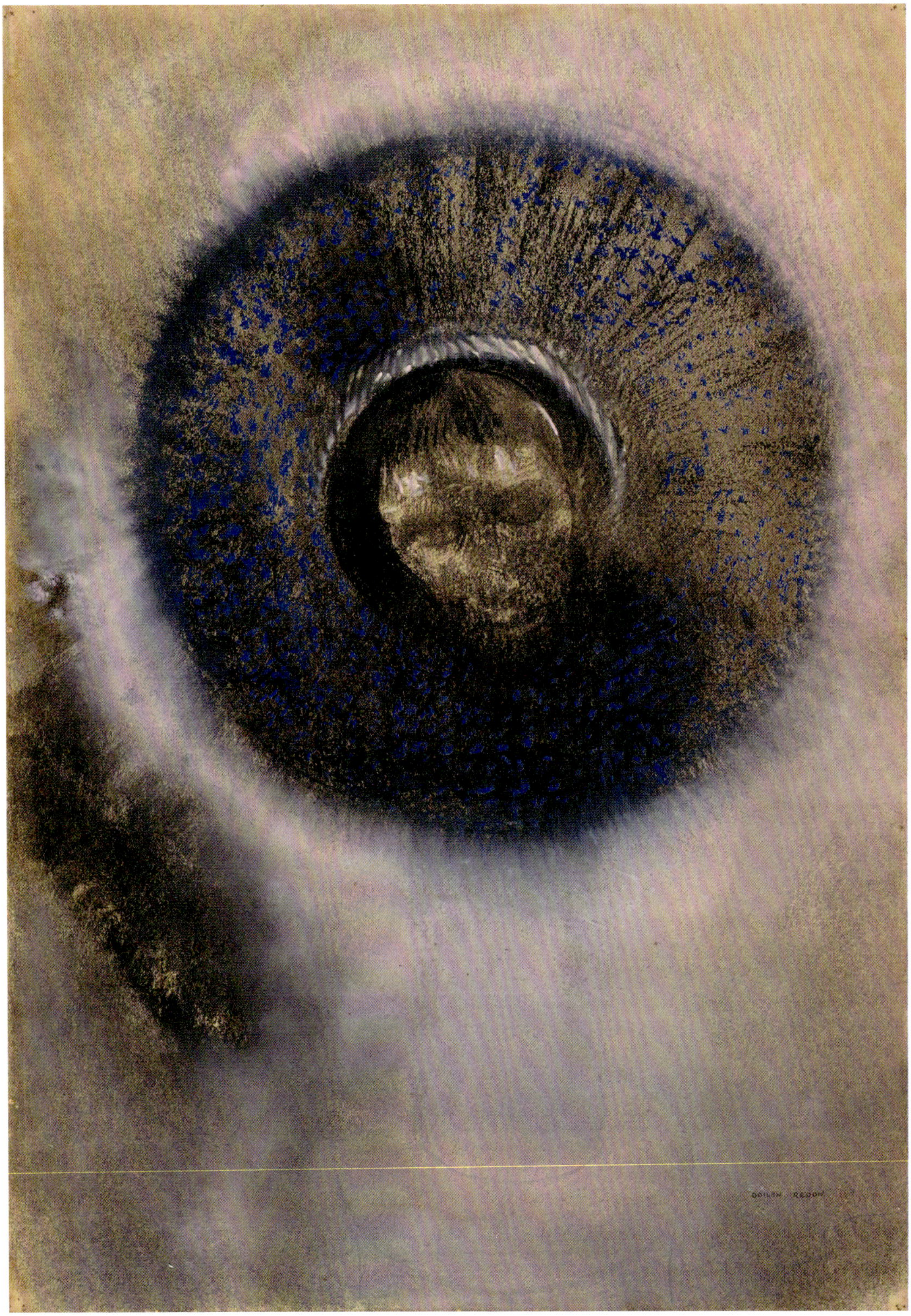

38

Head Within an Aureole, ca. 1894–95

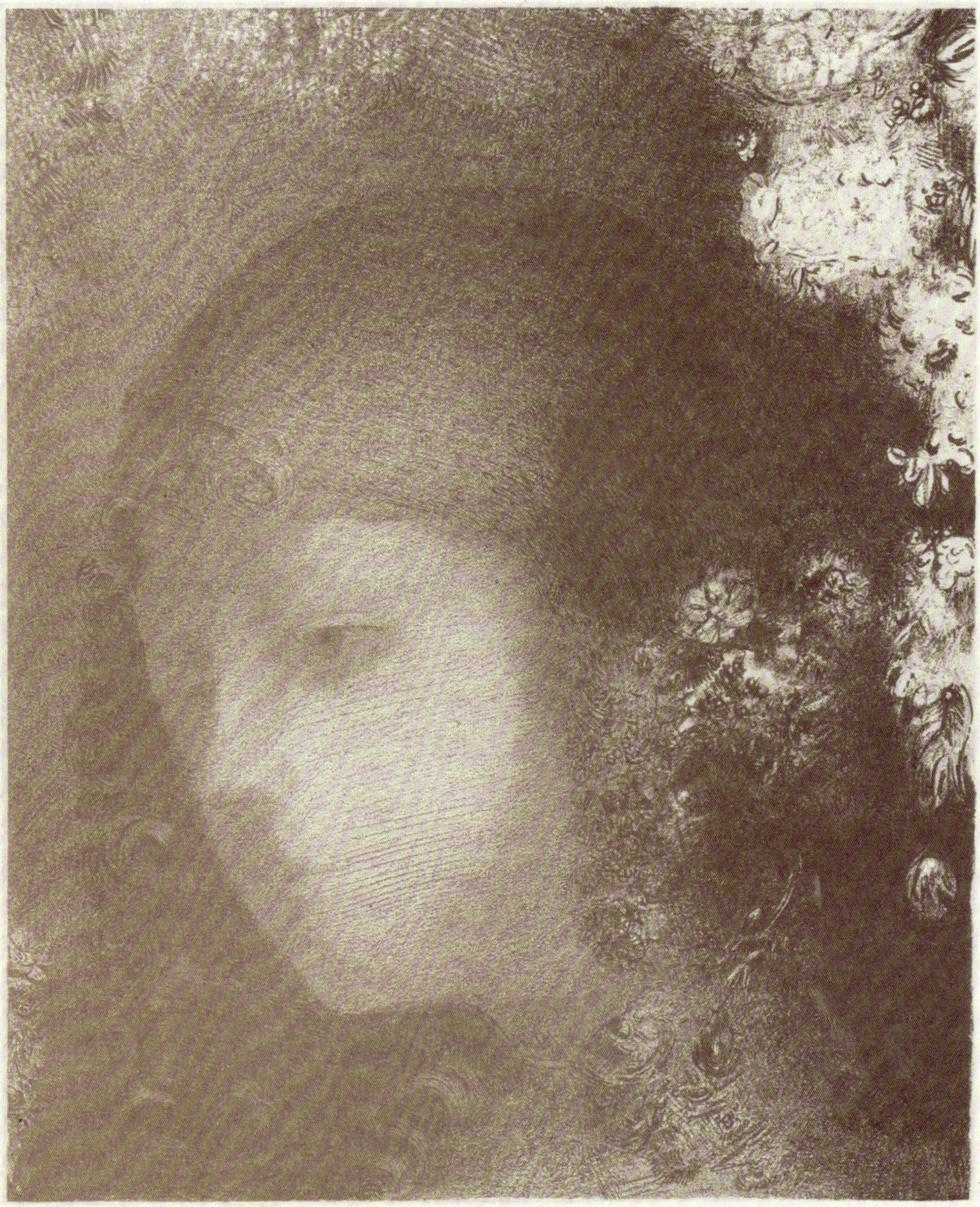

39
Head of a Child with Flowers, 1897

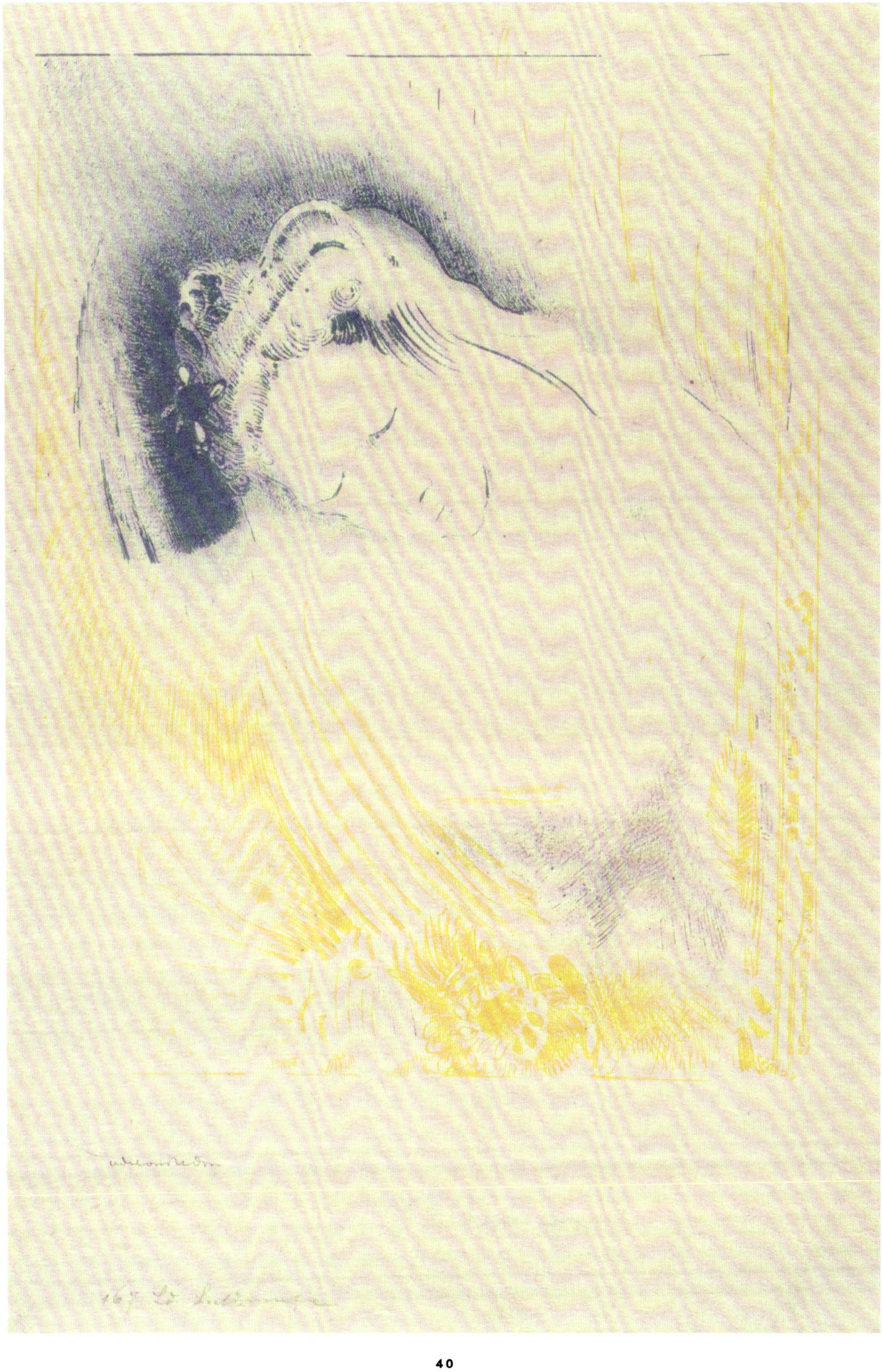

40
The Shulamite, 1897

41
Beatrice, 1897

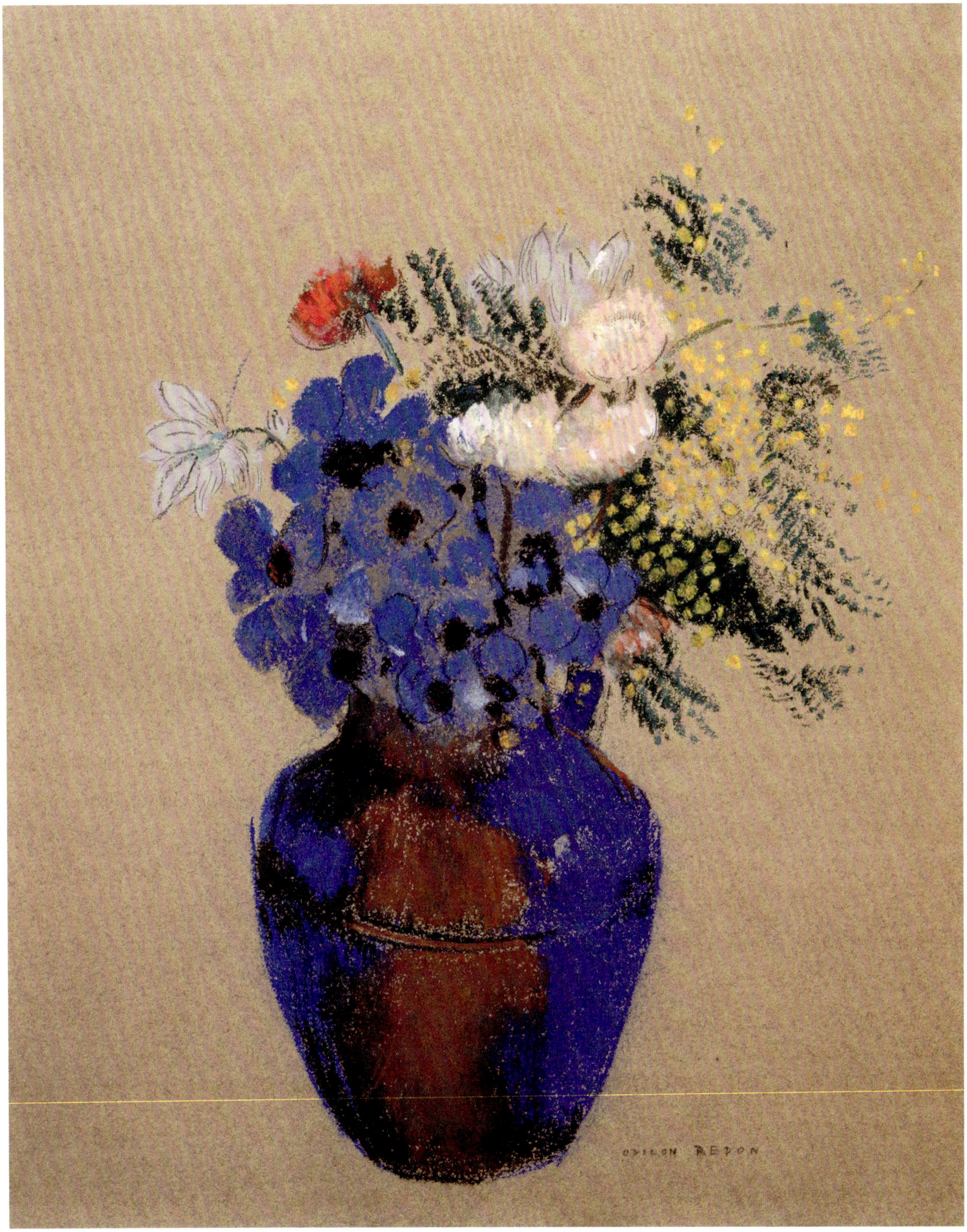

42
Vase of Flowers, ca. 1900–1905

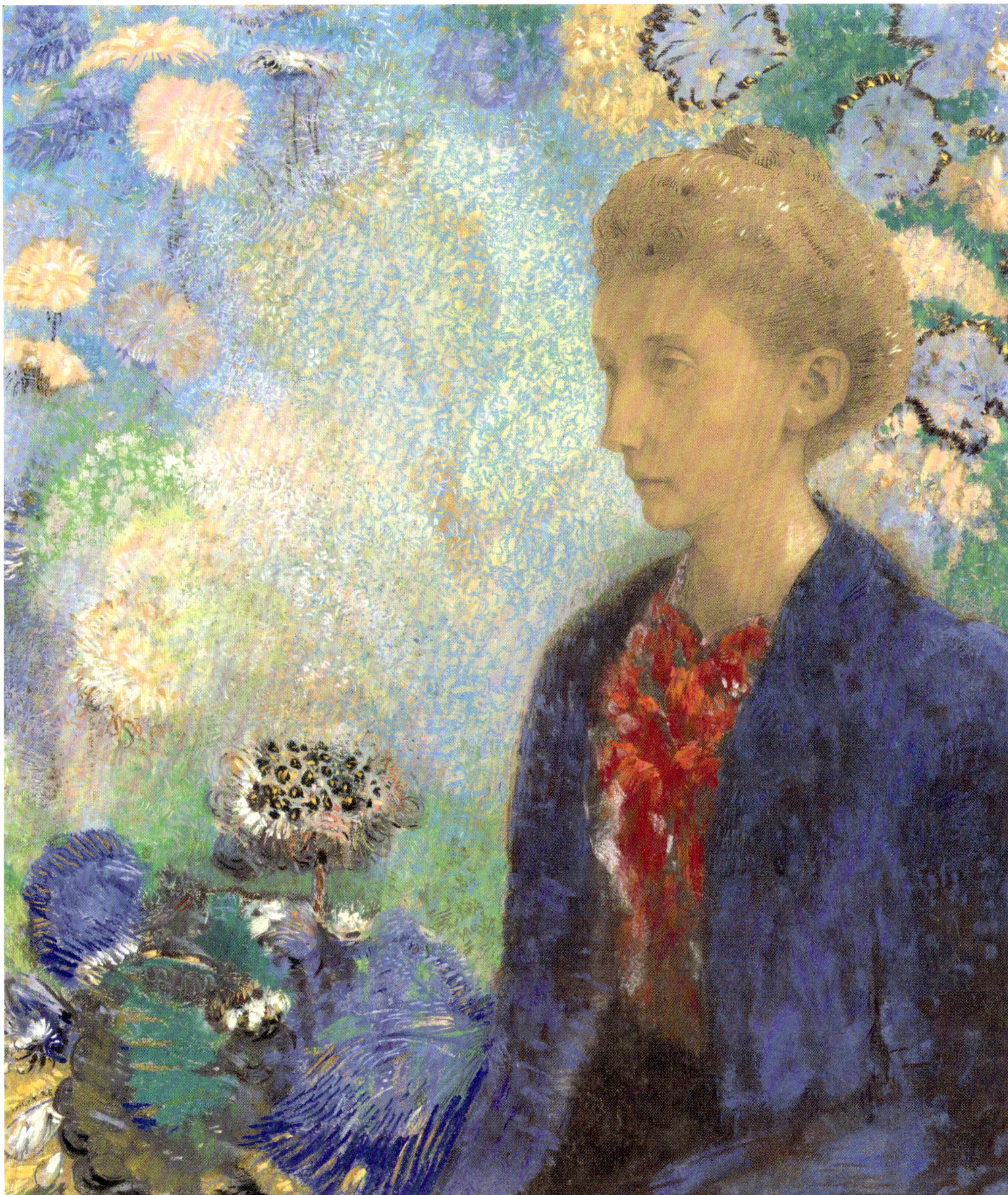

43
Baronne de Domecy, ca. 1900

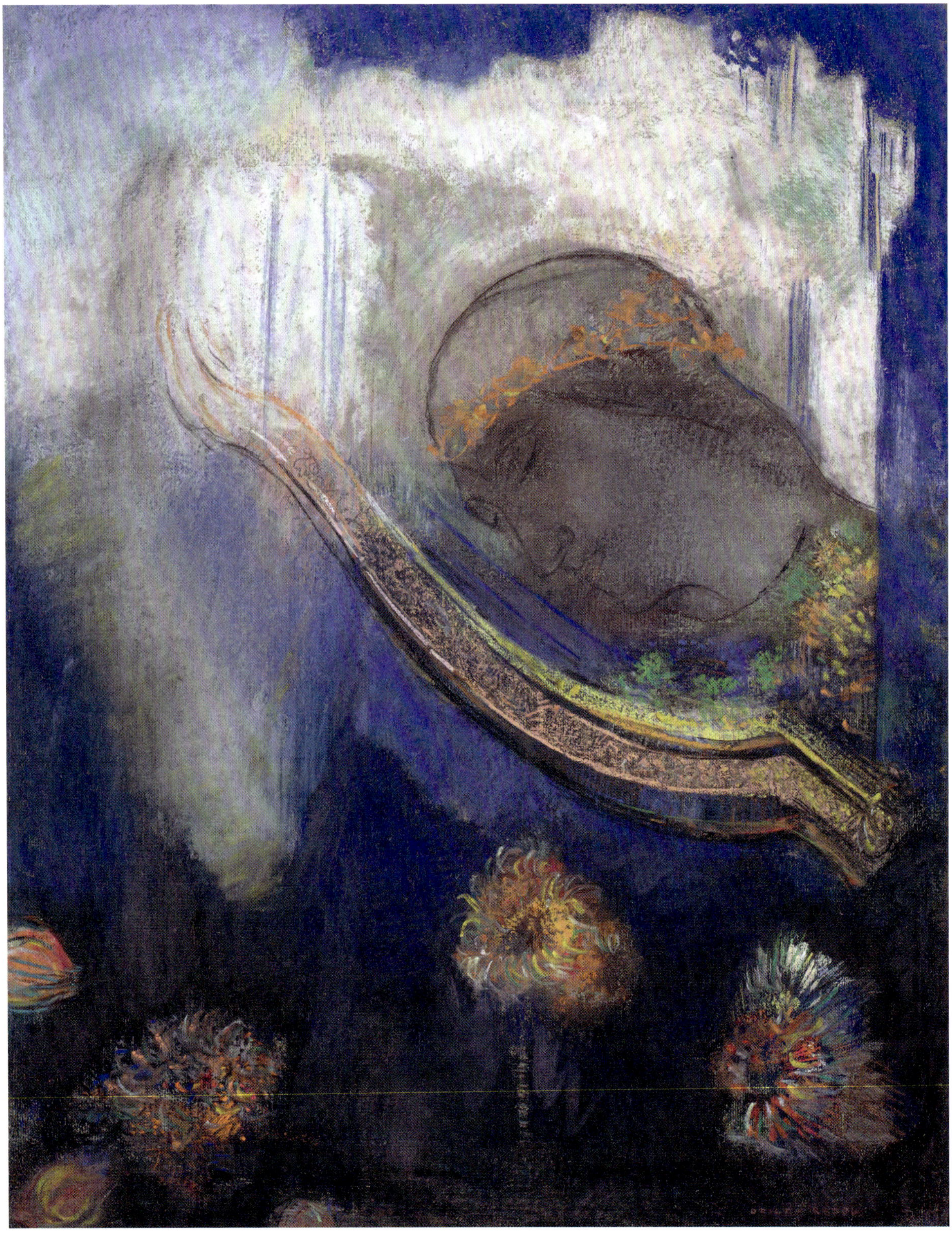

44
Orpheus, ca. 1905

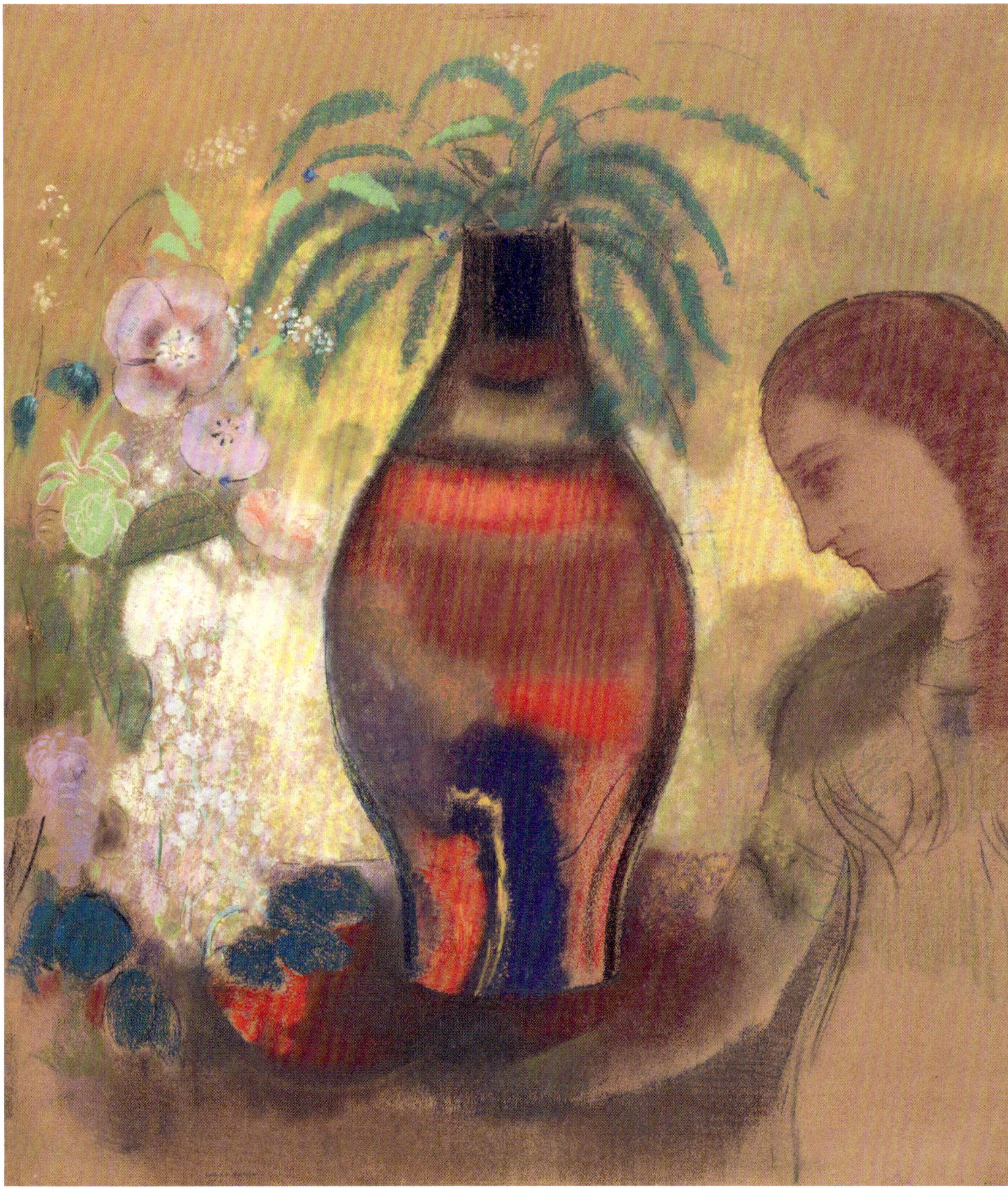

45
Vase of Flowers—Large Composition, 1913

Checklist of the Exhibition

All works are by Odilon Redon. Numbers correspond to the plates. Publisher information included when known. Original French titles provided in parentheses unless the work is traditionally known by an English title.

1
Apparition (*Apparition*), ca. 1880–90
Charcoal, powdered charcoal, black chalk, and black and yellow pastel, with stumping, on brown paper
52.5 × 37.3 cm (20 11/16 × 14 11/16 in.)
Los Angeles, J. Paul Getty Museum, 2013.38

2
The Battle of the Bones (*La bataille des os*), ca. 1881
Charcoal and pastel with stumping and removal on tan paper
36.5 × 45 cm (14 3/8 × 17 11/16 in.)
Los Angeles, J. Paul Getty Museum, 2024.17

3
The Tell-Tale Heart (*Le coeur révélateur*), 1883
Charcoal on brown paper
40 × 33.3 cm (15 3/4 × 13 1/8 in.)
Santa Barbara Museum of Art, Museum purchase, 1959.39

4
Christ, 1887
Lithograph on chine appliqué
Image: 33 × 27 cm (13 × 10 5/8 in.)
Fine Arts Museums of San Francisco, Bequest of Margaret Elsner, 1997.134
Printer: Lemercier et Cie, Paris
Edition: 25

5
Light (*Lumière*), 1893
Lithograph on chine appliqué
62.3 × 44.5 cm (24 1/2 × 17 1/2 in.)
Los Angeles, Getty Research Institute, 2011.PR.25
Printer: Becquet, Paris
Edition: 50

6
Old Knight (*Vieux chevalier*), 1896
From *The Album of Painter-Printmakers* (*L'album des peintres-graveurs*)
Lithograph on chine appliqué
56.8 × 43 cm (22 3/8 × 16 15/16 in.)
Los Angeles, Getty Research Institute, 2014.PR.6
Printer: Blanchard, Paris
Publisher: Vollard, Paris
Proof impression, outside the edition of 100

7
Cover of *Temptation of Saint Anthony* (*Tentation de Saint-Antoine*) (first series), 1888
Lithograph
Folded sheet: 44.5 × 31.6 cm (17 1/2 × 12 7/16 in.)
Los Angeles, Getty Research Institute, 2011.PR.30.11
Printer: Becquet, Paris
Publisher: Edmond Deman, Brussels
Portfolio edition: 60 announced, 58 printed

8
First a Pool of Water, Then a Prostitute, the Corner of a Temple, a Soldier's Face, a Chariot with Two White, Rearing Horses (*D'abord une flaque d'eau, ensuite une prostituée, le coin d'un temple, une figure de soldat, un char avec deux chevaux blancs qui se cabrent*), 1888
Plate I from the portfolio *Temptation of Saint Anthony* (*Tentation de Saint-Antoine*) (first series)
Lithograph on chine appliqué
44.9 × 31.8 cm (17 11/16 × 12 1/2 in.)
Los Angeles, Getty Research Institute, 2011.PR.30.1

9
It Is the Devil, Bearing Beneath His Two Wings the Seven Deadly Sins (*C'est le diable, portant sous ses deux ailes les sept péchés capitaux*), 1888
Plate II from the portfolio *Temptation of Saint Anthony* (*Tentation de Saint-Antoine*) (first series)
Lithograph on chine appliqué
44.9 × 31.8 cm (17 11/16 × 12 1/2 in.)
Los Angeles, Getty Research Institute, 2011.PR.30.2

10
And a Large Bird, Descending from the Sky, Hurls Itself Against the Topmost Point of Her Hair (*Et un grand oiseau, qui descend du ciel, vient s'abattre sur le sommet de sa chevelure*), 1888
Plate III from the portfolio *Temptation of Saint Anthony* (*Tentation de Saint-Antoine*) (first series)
Lithograph on chine appliqué
44.9 × 31.8 cm (17 11/16 × 12 1/2 in.)
Los Angeles, Getty Research Institute, 2011.PR.30.3

11
He Raises the Bronze Urn (*Il hausse le vase d'airain*), 1888
Plate IV from the portfolio *Temptation of Saint Anthony* (*Tentation de Saint-Antoine*) (first series)
Lithograph on chine appliqué
44.9 × 31.8 cm (17 11/16 × 12 1/2 in.)
Los Angeles, Getty Research Institute, 2011.PR.30.4

12
Then There Appears a Singular Being, Having the Head of a Man on the Body of a Fish (*Ensuite, parait un être singulier, ayant une tête d'homme sur un corps de poisson*), 1888
Plate V from the portfolio *Temptation of Saint Anthony* (*Tentation de Saint-Antoine*) (first series)
Lithograph on chine appliqué
44.9 × 31.8 cm (17 11/16 × 12 1/2 in.)
Los Angeles, Getty Research Institute, 2011.PR.30.5

13
It Is a Skull Wreathed with Roses. It Dominates a Woman's Torso of Pearly Whiteness (*C'est une tête de mort, avec une couronne de roses. Elle domine un torse de femme d'une blancheur nacrée*), 1888
Plate VI from the portfolio *Temptation of Saint Anthony* (*Tentation de Saint-Antoine*) (first series)
Lithograph on chine appliqué
44.9 × 31.8 cm (17 11/16 × 12 1/2 in.)
Los Angeles, Getty Research Institute, 2011.PR.30.6

14
The Chimera with Green Eyes Turns, Bays (*La Chimère aux yeux verts, tournoie, aboie*), 1888
Plate VII from the portfolio *Temptation of Saint Anthony* (*Tentation de Saint-Antoine*) (first series)
Lithograph on chine appliqué
44.9 × 31.8 cm (17 11/16 × 12 1/2 in.)
Los Angeles, Getty Research Institute, 2011.PR.30.7

15
And All Manner of Frightful Creatures Arise (*Et toutes sortes de bêtes effroyables surgissent*), 1888

Plate VIII from the portfolio *Temptation of Saint Anthony* (*Tentation de Saint-Antoine*) (first series)
Lithograph on chine appliqué
44.9 × 31.8 cm (17 11/16 × 12 1/2 in.)
Los Angeles, Getty Research Institute, 2011.PR.30.8

16
Everywhere Eyeballs Are Aflame (*Partout des prunelles flamboient*), 1888
Plate IX from the portfolio *Temptation of Saint Anthony* (*Tentation de Saint-Antoine*) (first series)
Lithograph on chine appliqué
44.9 × 31.8 cm (17 11/16 × 12 1/2 in.)
Los Angeles, Getty Research Institute, 2011.PR.30.9

17
And in the Very Disk of the Sun Shines the Face of Jesus Christ (*Et dans le disque même du soleil, rayonne la face de Jésus-Christ*), 1888
Plate X from the portfolio *Temptation of Saint Anthony* (*Tentation de Saint-Antoine*) (first series)
Lithograph on chine appliqué
44.9 × 31.8 cm (17 11/16 × 12 1/2 in.)
Los Angeles, Getty Research Institute, 2011.PR.30.10

18
Cover of *Dreams* (*Songes*), 1891
Lithograph
Folded sheet: 45.9 × 32.3 cm (18 1/16 × 12 3/4 in.)
Los Angeles, Getty Research Institute, 2013.PR.52.7
Printer: Becquet, Paris
Portfolio edition: 80

19
It Was a Veil, an Imprint (*C'était un voile, une empreinte*), 1891
Lithograph on chine appliqué
Plate I from the portfolio *Dreams* (*Songes*)
44.8 × 31.5 cm (17 5/8 × 12 3/8 in.)
Los Angeles, Getty Research Institute, 2013.PR.52.1

20
And Beyond, the Astral Idol, the Apotheosis (*Et là-bas l'idole astrale, l'apothéose*), 1891
Plate II from the portfolio *Dreams* (*Songes*)
Lithograph on chine appliqué
44.8 × 31.5 cm (17 5/8 × 12 3/8 in.)
Los Angeles, Getty Research Institute, 2013.PR.52.2

21
Precarious Glimmering, a Head Suspended in Infinity (*Lueur précaire, une tête à l'infini suspendue*), 1891
Plate III from the portfolio *Dreams* (*Songes*)
Lithograph on chine appliqué
44.8 × 31.5 cm (17 5/8 × 12 3/8 in.)
Los Angeles, Getty Research Institute, 2013.PR.52.3

22
Beneath the Wing of Shadow the Black Creature Was Biting Energetically (*Sous l'aile d'ombre, l'être noir appliquait une active morsure*), 1891
Plate IV from the portfolio *Dreams* (*Songes*)
Lithograph on chine appliqué
44.8 × 31.5 cm (17 5/8 × 12 3/8 in.)
Los Angeles, Getty Research Institute, 2013.PR.52.4

23
Pilgrim of the Sublunary World (*Pélerin du monde sublunaire*), 1891
Plate V from the portfolio *Dreams* (*Songes*)
Lithograph on chine appliqué
44.8 × 31.5 cm (17 5/8 × 12 3/8 in.)
Los Angeles, Getty Research Institute, 2013.PR.52.5

24
Day (*Le jour*), 1891
Plate VI from the portfolio *Dreams* (*Songes*)
Lithograph on chine appliqué
44.8 × 31.5 cm (17 5/8 × 12 3/8 in.)
Los Angeles, Getty Research Institute, 2013.PR.52.6

25
Cover of *Apocalypse of Saint John* (*Apocalypse de Saint-Jean*), 1899
Lithograph
Folded sheet: 62.7 × 44.3 cm (24 11/16 × 17 7/16 in.)
Los Angeles, Getty Research Institute, 2013.PR.4.13
Printer: Blanchard, Paris
Publisher: Vollard, Paris
Portfolio edition: 100

26
And He Had in His Right Hand Seven Stars; and Out of His Mouth Went a Sharp Two-Edged Sword (*Et il avait en sa main droite sept étoiles, et de sa bouche sortait une épée aigüe à deux tranchants*), 1899
Plate I from the portfolio *Apocalypse of Saint John* (*Apocalypse de Saint-Jean*)
Lithograph on chine appliqué
56.4 × 42.5 cm (22 3/16 × 16 3/4 in.)
Los Angeles, Getty Research Institute, 2013.PR.4.1

27
And I Saw in the Right Hand of Him That Sat on the Throne a Book Written Within and on the Backside, Sealed with Seven Seals (*Puis je vis dans la main droite de celui qui était assis sur le trône, un livre écrit dedans et dehors, scellé de sept sceaux*), 1899
Plate II from the portfolio *Apocalypse of Saint John* (*Apocalypse de Saint-Jean*)
Lithograph on chine appliqué
56.4 × 42.5 cm (22 3/16 × 16 3/4 in.)
Los Angeles, Getty Research Institute, 2013.PR.4.2

28
And His Name That Sat on Him Was Death (*Et celui qui était monté dessus se nommait la Mort*), 1899
Plate III from the portfolio *Apocalypse of Saint John* (*Apocalypse de Saint-Jean*)
Lithograph on chine appliqué
56.4 × 42.5 cm (22 3/16 × 16 3/4 in.)
Los Angeles, Getty Research Institute, 2013.PR.4.3

29
And the Angel Took the Censer (*Puis l'ange prit l'encensoir*), 1899
Plate IV from the portfolio *Apocalypse of Saint John* (*Apocalypse de Saint-Jean*)
Lithograph on chine appliqué
56.4 × 42.5 cm (22 3/16 × 16 3/4 in.)
Los Angeles, Getty Research Institute, 2013.PR.4.4

30
And There Fell a Great Star from Heaven, Burning as It Were a Lamp (*Et il tomba du ciel une grande étoile, ardente comme un flambeau*), 1899
Plate V from the portfolio *Apocalypse of Saint John* (*Apocalypse de Saint-Jean*)
Lithograph on chine appliqué
56.4 × 42.5 cm (22 3/16 × 16 3/4 in.)
Los Angeles, Getty Research Institute, 2013.PR.4.5

31
A Woman Clothed with the Sun (*Une femme revêtue du Soleil*), 1899
Plate VI from the portfolio *Apocalypse of Saint John* (*Apocalypse de Saint-Jean*)
Lithograph on chine appliqué
56.4 × 42.5 cm (22 3/16 × 16 3/4 in.)
Los Angeles, Getty Research Institute, 2013.PR.4.6

32
And Another Angel Came Out of the Temple Which Is in Heaven, and He Also Having a Sharp Sickle (*Et un autre ange sortit du temple qui est au ciel, ayant lui aussi une faucille tranchante*), 1899
Plate VII from the portfolio *Apocalypse of Saint John* (*Apocalypse de Saint-Jean*)
Lithograph on chine appliqué
56.4 × 42.5 cm (22 3/16 × 16 3/4 in.)
Los Angeles, Getty Research Institute, 2013.PR.4.7

33
And I Saw an Angel Coming Down from Heaven, Having the Key of the Bottomless Pit and a Great Chain in His Hand (*Après cela, je vis descendre du ciel un ange qui avait la clef de l'abîme, et une grande chaîne en sa main*), 1899
Plate VIII from the portfolio *Apocalypse of Saint John* (*Apocalypse de Saint-Jean*)
Lithograph on chine appliqué
56.4 × 42.5 cm (22 3/16 × 16 3/4 in.)
Los Angeles, Getty Research Institute, 2013.PR.4.8

34
And Bound Him a Thousand Years (*Et le lia pour mille ans*), 1899
Plate IX from the portfolio *Apocalypse of Saint John* (*Apocalypse de Saint-Jean*)
Lithograph on chine appliqué
56.4 × 42.5 cm (22 3/16 × 16 3/4 in.)
Los Angeles, Getty Research Institute, 2013.PR.4.9

35
And the Devil That Deceived Them Was Cast into the Lake Fire and Brimstone, Where the Beast and the False Prophet Are (*Et le diable qui les séduisait, fut jeté dans l'étang de feu et de soufre, où est la bête et le faux prophète*), 1899
Plate X from the portfolio *Apocalypse of Saint John* (*Apocalypse de Saint-Jean*)
Lithograph on chine appliqué
56.4 × 42.5 cm (22 3/16 × 16 3/4 in.)
Los Angeles, Getty Research Institute, 2013.PR.4.10

36
And I, John, Saw the Holy City, New Jerusalem, Coming Down from God and Out of Heaven (*Et moi Jean, je vis la sainte cité, la nouvelle Jérusalem, qui descendait du Ciel, d'auprès de Dieu*), 1899
Plate XI from the portfolio *Apocalypse of Saint John* (*Apocalypse de Saint-Jean*)
Lithograph on chine appliqué
56.4 × 42.5 cm (22 3/16 × 16 3/4 in.)
Los Angeles, Getty Research Institute, 2013.PR.4.11

37
And I, John, Saw These Things, and Heard Them (*C'est moi, Jean, qui ai vu et qui ai ouï ces choses*), 1899
Plate XII from the portfolio *Apocalypse of Saint John* (*Apocalypse de Saint-Jean*)
Lithograph on chine appliqué
56.4 × 42.5 cm (22 3/16 × 16 3/4 in.)
Los Angeles, Getty Research Institute, 2013.PR.4.12

38
Head Within an Aureole (*Tête auréolée*), ca. 1894–95
Charcoal and pastel with stumping on pink paper (now discolored)
52 × 36 cm (20 1/2 × 14 3/16 in.)
Los Angeles, J. Paul Getty Museum, 2016.10

39
Head of a Child with Flowers (*Tête d'enfant avec fleurs*), 1897
Lithograph in brown
56.8 × 38.7 cm (22 3/8 × 15 1/4 in.)
Los Angeles, Hammer Museum, Collection UCLA Grunwald Center for the Graphic Arts, Gift of Mr. and Mrs. Fred Grunwald, 1956.5.96
Printer: Lemercier et Cie, Paris
Publisher: Gustave Pellet, Paris
Proof impression, outside the edition of 50

40
The Shulamite (*La Sulamite*), 1897
Color lithograph
32.1 × 22.2 cm (12 5/8 × 8 3/4 in.)
Los Angeles, Hammer Museum, Collection of UCLA Grunwald Center for the Graphic Arts, Bequest of Elisabeth Dean, 2025.12.415
Printer: Auguste Clot, Paris
Publisher: Gustave Pellet, Paris
Edition: 50

41
Beatrice (*Béatrice*), 1897
From *The Album of Original Prints from the Vollard Gallery* (*L'album d'estampes originales de la Galerie Vollard*)
Color lithograph on chine appliqué
52 × 42.6 cm (20 1/2 × 16 3/4 in.)
Fine Arts Museums of San Francisco, Museum Purchase, Achenbach Foundation for Graphic Arts Endowment Fund, 1971.29.2
Printer: Auguste Clot, Paris
Publisher: Vollard, Paris
Edition: 100

42
Vase of Flowers, ca. 1900–1905
Pastel
39.7 × 33 cm (15 5/8 × 13 in.)
Los Angeles, Hammer Museum, The Armand Hammer Collection, Gift of Dr. Armand Hammer, AH.91.31

43
Baronne de Domecy, ca. 1900
Pastel and graphite on light brown paper
61 × 42.4 cm (24 × 16 11/16 in.)
Los Angeles, J. Paul Getty Museum, 2005.1

44
Orpheus, ca. 1905
Pastel on gray laid paper, affixed to canvas mount
59.5 × 46.8 cm (23 7/16 × 18 7/16 in.)
Fine Arts Museums of San Francisco, Bequest of Frederick J. Hellman, 1965.29

45
Vase of Flowers—Large Composition, 1913
Pastel
72.7 x 64.5 cm (28 5/8 × 25 3/8 in.)
Los Angeles County Museum of Art, Mr. and Mrs. George Gard De Sylva Collection, M.46.3.1

Acknowledgments

The exhibition *Odilon Redon: Otherworldly Visions* is largely centered on the rich collections of the J. Paul Getty Museum and the Getty Research Institute, and was realized through the support of wonderful colleagues within these institutions and beyond.

I would like to express my gratitude to Natalia Lauricella, curator of prints and drawings at the Achenbach Foundation for Graphic Arts at the Fine Arts Museums of San Francisco, for her contribution to this catalogue. Her thorough investigation of Redon's printmaking practice deepened my understanding of the artist's techniques and enriched the exhibition.

For their overarching support of the exhibition at the Getty Museum, I would like to thank Timothy Potts, Maria Hummer-Tuttle and Robert Tuttle Director; Richard Rand, associate director for collections; and Heidi Domine Strean, associate director for exhibitions. This project would not have been possible without the guidance of Julian Brooks, senior curator of drawings, who helped me to navigate the exhibition and publication processes. In the Department of Drawings, I would also like to thank Stephanie Schrader, Edina Adam, Casey Lee, and Michelle Ross, as well as former interns Drew Lash, Flavia Barbarini, and Jonathan Hayden, for their encouragement and assistance. I am indebted to Michelle Sullivan and Victoria Binder in the Department of Paper Conservation for their valuable insights into objects and materials.

Through the addition of a small group of critical loans, the exhibition highlights the strengths of nineteenth-century French art in California museums. I am grateful to my colleagues at these local institutions who made their collections accessible and helped to facilitate loans, including Furio Rinaldi and Cyntia Karnes at the Fine Arts Museums of San Francisco; Naoko Takahatake, Jennie Waldow, and Kelin Michael at the Hammer Museum; Britt Salvesen, Claire Spadafora Baes, Soko Furuhata, and Amanda Burr at the Los Angeles County Museum of Art; and James Glisson and Kelsey McGinnis at the Santa Barbara Museum of Art. I also want to express my appreciation to my colleagues at the Getty Research Institute. Thanks to conservator Elyse Driscoll and the staff of the Special Collections Reading Room for their assistance in consulting the collection.

The exhibition was brought to life by the diligent work of colleagues across the Getty Museum. I would like to thank head of exhibitions Amber Keller, exhibition coordinator Susan McGinty, designers Chaya Arabia and Leah McCloskey, editor Sheila Flaherty-Jones, Spanish-language editor Iliana Alcántar, interpretive content specialist Maite Alvarez, registrar Amy Weiss, senior mountmaker David McDaniel, and the team of preparators under Michael Mitchell and Nicholas McCullough for their essential contributions to the display.

I am grateful to the extended Getty Publications team for their tireless work on the production of the present catalogue, including publisher Kara Kirk, editor in chief Nina Wiener, former editor in chief Diana Murphy, managing editor Nola Butler, manuscript and project editor Nikki Bazar, senior editor Ruth Evans Lane, production manager Michelle Deemer, designer Jon Grizzle, rights coordinator Danielle Brink, proofreader Dianne Woo, and indexer Michael Goldstein. I would also like to thank Michael Smith and his team in Imaging Studios for their contributions to this project.

This exhibition and catalogue build upon a rich body of literature on the art and life of Odilon Redon, and I am indebted to the many scholars whose work has informed my research. I would particularly like to acknowledge Lee Hendrix, former senior curator of drawings at the Getty Museum, whose exhibition and catalogue *Noir: The Romance of Black in 19th-Century French Drawings and Prints* provided a critical foundation of expertise on Redon's drawings and prints in the Getty collections. I am also grateful to paper conservator Harriet Stratis for generously sharing her knowledge of Redon's materials and techniques.

Finally, I would like to thank my family and friends who supported me through never-ending discussions of pastel, charcoal, and floating eyeballs, with special appreciation for my favorite research assistant, Charlie.

Danielle Canter

Bibliography

BACOU 1956 Bacou, Roseline. *Odilon Redon*. 2 vols. Pierre Cailler, 1956.

BACOU 1960 Bacou, Roseline, ed. *Lettres de Gauguin, Gide, Huysmans, Jammes, Mallarmé, Verhaeren … à Odilon Redon*. J. Corti, 1960.

BACOU 1987 Bacou, Roseline. *Odilon Redon: Pastels*. Translated by Beatrice Rehl. George Braziller, 1987.

BANN 2001 Bann, Stephen. *Parallel Lines: Printmakers, Painters, and Photographers in Nineteenth-Century France*. Yale University Press, 2001.

BERGE, KEIJER, AND MEEDENDORP 2002 Berge, Jos ten, Kees Keijer, and Teio Meedendorp. *Hommes de Valeur: Henri Fantin-Latour, Odilon Redon en Tijdgenoten*. Waanders, 2002.

BERGER 1964 Berger, Klaus. *Odilon Redon: Fantasy and Colour*. Translated by Michael Bullock. Weidenfeld and Nicolson, 1964.

BLACK 2010 Black, Candice, ed. *Odilon Redon: I Am the First Consciousness of Chaos: The Black Album*. Solar, 2010.

BOUCHOR 1880 Bouchor, Maurice. "La bataille des os: Nouvelle fantastique." In *Contes parisiens en vers*. Charpentier, 1880.

BOUVIER 2014 Bouvier, Raphaël, ed. *Odilon Redon*. Exh. cat. Fondation Beyeler, 2014.

BUCHANAN AND MACIEJUNES 1990 Buchanan, John E., and Nannette V. Maciejunes. *Odilon Redon: The Ian Woodner Family Collection*. Exh. cat. Dixon Gallery and Gardens, 1990.

CLEMENT 1996 Clement, Russell T. *Four French Symbolists: A Sourcebook on Pierre Puvis de Chavannes, Gustave Moreau, Odilon Redon, and Maurice Denis*. Greenwood, 1996.

DALY ET AL. 2019 Daly, Nathan S., Michelle Sullivan, Lynn Lee, John K. Delaney, and Karen Trentelman. "Odilon Redon's Noir Drawings: Characterization of Materials and Methods Using Noninvasive Imaging and Spectroscopies." *Heritage Science* 7, no. 43 (2019): 1–13.

DESTRÉE 1891 Destrée, Jules. *L'oeuvre lithographique de Odilon Redon, catalogue descriptif*. E. Deman, 1891.

DI STEFANO 2005 Di Stefano, Eva. *Redon*. Giunti, 2005.

DRUICK 1994 Druick, Douglas W., ed. *Odilon Redon: Prince of Dreams, 1840–1916*. Exh. cat. Art Institute of Chicago; Van Gogh Museum; Royal Academy of Arts; with Harry N. Abrams, 1994.

DRUICK AND ZEGERS 1994A Druick, Douglas W., and Peter Kort Zegers. "In the Public Eye, 1879–1889." In Druick 1994.

DRUICK AND ZEGERS 1994B Druick, Douglas W., and Peter Kort Zegers. "Painful Origins." In Druick 1994.

DRUICK AND ZEGERS 1994C Druick, Douglas W., and Peter Kort Zegers. "Taking Wing, 1870–1878." In Druick 1994.

EISENMAN 1984 Eisenman, Stephen F. "On the Politics of Dreams: A Study of the *Noirs* of Odilon Redon." PhD diss., Princeton University, 1984.

EISENMAN 1990 Eisenman, Stephen F. *Le Fantastique Réel: Graphic Works by Odilon Redon*. Exh. cat. Katonah Museum of Art, 1990.

EISENMAN 1992 Eisenman, Stephen [F.]. *The Temptation of Saint Redon: Biography, Ideology, and Style in the Noirs of Odilon Redon*. University of Chicago Press, 1992.

FIGURA 2005 Figura, Starr. "Redon and the Lithographed Portfolio." In Hauptman 2005.

FLAMENT 1905 Flament, Albert. "Le Salon d'automne." *La Presse*, October 18, 1905.

FLAUBERT 1874 Flaubert, Gustave. *La tentation de Saint Antoine*. Charpentier, 1874.

GAMBONI 2002 Gamboni, Dario. "Redon, Ensor, Seurat." In *Potential Images: Ambiguity and Indeterminacy in Modern Art*, translated by Mark Treharne. Reaktion, 2002.

GAMBONI 2011 Gamboni, Dario. *The Brush and the Pen: Odilon Redon and Literature*. Translated by Mary Whittall. University of Chicago Press, 2011.

GAMBONI, HOUSSAIS, AND PINCHON 2022 Gamboni, Dario, Laurent Houssais, and Pierre Pinchon. *Redon retrouvé: Oeuvres et documents inédits*. Cohen & Cohen, 2022.

GILMOUR 1988 Gilmour, Pat. "Cher Monsieur Clot … Auguste Clot and His Role as a Colour Lithographer." In *Lasting Impressions: Lithography as an Art*, edited by Pat Gilmour. University of Pennsylvania Press, 1988.

GIVISKOS 2018 Giviskos, Christine. *Set in Stone: Lithography in Paris, 1815–1900*. Hirmer, 2018.

GOTT 1990A Gott, Ted. "Courting the Stone: Redon's Lithographic Techniques." In Gott 1990B.

GOTT 1990B Gott, Ted. *The Enchanted Stone: The Graphic Worlds of Odilon Redon*. Exh. cat. National Gallery of Victoria, 1990.

GOTT 1990C Gott, Ted. "Marriage in the Workshop: The Printer as Partner." In Gott 1990B.

HARRISON 1986 Harrison, Sharon R. *The Etchings of Odilon Redon: A Catalogue Raisonné*. Da Capo, 1986.

HAUPTMAN 2005 Hauptman, Jodi. *Beyond the Visible: The Art of Odilon Redon*. With essays by Marina van Zuylen, Starr Figura, and Tricia YunJoo Paik. Exh. cat. Museum of Modern Art, 2005.

HENDRIX 2016 Hendrix, Lee, ed. *Noir: The Romance of Black in 19th-Century French Drawings and Prints*. Exh. cat. J. Paul Getty Museum, 2016.

HOBBS 1977 Hobbs, Richard. *Odilon Redon*. New York Graphic Society, 1977.

HOMBURG 2018 Homburg, Cornelia, ed. *Odilon Redon: Literature and Music*. Exh. cat. Ny Carlsberg Glyptotek, 2018.

HUYSMANS 1884 Huysmans, Joris-Karl. *À rebours*. Charpentier, 1884.

HYMAN 2001 Hyman, Alan, ed. *Odilon Redon: Les Estampes—The Graphic Work, Catalogue Raisonné*. Alan Wofsy Fine Arts, 2001.

JENSEN 1994 Jensen, Robert. *Marketing Modernism in Fin-de-Siècle Europe*. Princeton University Press, 1994.

JIRAT-WASIUTYŃSKI 1992 Jirat-Wasiutyński, Vojtěch. "The Charcoal Drawings of Odilon Redon." In *Drawing: Masters and Methods, Raphael to Redon*, edited by Diana Dethloff. Philip Wilson, 1992.

KALBA 2017 Kalba, Laura Anne. "Chromolithography: Posters, Trade Cards, and the Politics of Ephemera Collecting in Fin-de-Siècle France." In *Color in the Age of Impressionism: Commerce, Technology, and Art*. Pennsylvania State University Press, 2017.

LARSON 2005 Larson, Barbara. *The Dark Side of Nature: Science, Society, and the Fantastic in the Work of Odilon Redon*. Pennsylvania State University Press, 2005.

LAURICELLA 2022 Lauricella, Natalia P. "The Master Printer's Labor: Crafting the Color Art Lithograph in Fin-de-Siècle France." *Nouvelles de l'estampe* 267 (Spring 2022). https://doi.org/10.4000/estampe.2238.

LEEMAN 1994 Leeman, Fred. "Redon's Spiritualism and the Rise of Mysticism." In Druick 1994.

MAINARDI 1993 Mainardi, Patricia. *The End of the Salon: Art and the State in the Early Third Republic*. Cambridge University Press, 1993.

MAINARDI 2017 Mainardi, Patricia. *Another World: Nineteenth-Century Illustrated Print Culture*. Yale University Press, 2017.

MELLERIO 1898 Mellerio, André. "Exposition de la deuxième année de *L'album d'estampes originales*; Galerie Vollard, 6, rue Laffitte." *L'estampe et l'affiche* 1 (1898): 10–11.

MELLERIO 1913 Mellerio, André. *Odilon Redon*. Société pour l'Étude de la Gravure Française, 1913.

MELLERIO 1923 Mellerio, André. *Odilon Redon: Peintre, desinateur, et graveur*. Henri Floury, 1923.

MELLERIO 1978 [1898] Mellerio, André. *Original Color Lithography*. Translated by Margaret Needham. Reprinted in Phillip Dennis Cate and Sinclair Hamilton Hitchings, eds., *The Color Revolution: Color Lithography in France, 1890–1900*. Rutgers University Press, 1978. First published in 1898 by L'Estampe et l'Affiche.

NOCE 2011 Noce, Vincent. *Odilon Redon, dans l'oeil de Darwin*. Réunion des Musées Nationaux, 2011.

PARIS 1905 *Société du Salon d'Automne: Catalogue de peinture, sculpture, dessin, gravure, architecture et art décoratif*. Exh. cat. Compagnie Française des Papiers-Monnaie, 1905. https://www.aaa.si.edu/collections/items/detail/salon-d-automne-8797.

REDON 1923 Redon, Odilon. *Lettres d'Odilon Redon, 1878–1916*. G. Van Oest, 1923.

REDON 1961 [1869] Redon, Odilon. "Bresdin: Drawings on Stone, Etchings, Original Drawings." Translated by Alexander and Anne Hull, *Massachusetts Review* (Autumn 1960). Reprinted in *Odilon Redon, Gustave Moreau, Rodolphe Bresdin*. Exh. cat. Museum of Modern Art; with Art Institute of Chicago, 1961. First published in *La Gironde*, January 1, 1869.

REDON 1986 [1922] Redon, Odilon. *To Myself: Notes on Life, Art, and Artists*. Translated by Mira Jacob and Jeanne L. Wasserman. G. Braziller, 1986. First published in 1922 as *À soi-même, journal (1867–1915): Notes sur la vie, l'art et les artistes* by H. Floury.

REDON 1987 Redon, Odilon. *Lettres inédites d'Odilon Redon à Bonger*. Edited by Suzy Levy. J. Corti, 1987.

ROSEN 1988 Rosen, Jeffrey. "Lemercier et Compagnie: Photolithography and the Industrialization of Print Production in France, 1837–1859." PhD diss., Northwestern University, 1988.

SALÉ 2007 Salé, Marie-Pierre, ed. *Odilon Redon*. Exh. cat. Musée d'Orsay, 2007.

STRATIS 1994 Stratis, Harriet K. "Beneath the Surface: Redon's Methods and Materials." In Druick 1994.

STRATIS 1995 Stratis, Harriet K. "A Technical Investigation of Odilon Redon's Pastels and Noirs." *Book and Paper Group Annual* 14 (1995): 87–103.

STUFFMANN 2007 Stuffmann, Margret. "J'ai fait un art selon moi seul: The Exhibition." In Stuffmann and Hollein 2007.

STUFFMANN AND HOLLEIN 2007 Stuffmann, Margret, and Max Hollein, eds. *Odilon Redon: As in a Dream*. Exh. cat. Hatje Cantz, 2007.

TRAPP 1980 Trapp, Frank. *The Temptation of Saint Anthony by Odilon Redon*. Mead Art Museum, Amherst College, 1980.

VIALLA 1988 Vialla, Jean. *La vie et l'oeuvre d'Odilon Redon*. ACR Edition, 1988.

WILDENSTEIN 1992–98 Wildenstein, Alec. *Odilon Redon: Catalogue raisonné de l'oeuvre peint et dessiné*. 4 vols. Wildenstein Institute, 1992–98. https://wpi.art/2019/01/08/odilon-redon.

WILSON 1978 Wilson, Michael. *Nature and Imagination: The Work of Odilon Redon*. Dutton, 1978.

Illustration Credits

Figs. 1, 16: © RMN-Grand Palais / Art Resource, NY / Photo © Hervé Lewandowski
Fig. 3: © RMN-Grand Palais / Art Resource, NY / Photo: Michèle Bellot
Figs. 4, 27: The Art Institute of Chicago / Art Resource, NY
Figs. 5–6, 8, 11, 14: Digital Image © The Museum of Modern Art / Licensed by SCALA / Art Resource, NY
Fig. 7: metmuseum.org / CC0
Figs. 12, 25: Rijksmuseum, Amsterdam
Fig. 13: Digital Image © CNAC / MNAM, Dist. RMN-Grand Palais / Art Resource, NY / Photo © Hervé Lewandowski
Fig. 15: Photo: © 2026 Museum of Fine Arts, Boston
Fig. 18; plates 41, 44: Courtesy of the Fine Arts Museums of San Francisco
Fig. 19: Courtesy National Gallery of Art, Washington, DC
Figs. 20, 22; plate 4: Courtesy of the Fine Arts Museums of San Francisco / Photo: Jorge Bachman
Fig. 21: Image copyright © The Metropolitan Museum of Art. Image source: Art Resource, NY
Fig. 23: Van Gogh Museum, Amsterdam (State of the Netherlands)
Fig. 24: Carlo Bollo / Alamy
Fig. 26: Bibliothèque nationale de France
Plate 39: Photo: Jeff McLane
Plate 45: Photo © Museum Associates / LACMA Conservation Center, by Yosi Pozeilov

Index

Page numbers in *italics* refer to illustrations.